DOCTOR SATAN

A DESPICABLE TRUE STORY OF HOPE, EXPLOITATION, GREED AND MURDER

RYAN GREEN

For Helen, Harvey, Frankie and Dougie

Disclaimer

This book is about real people committing real crimes. The story has been constructed by facts but some of the scenes, dialogue and characters have been fictionalised.

Polite Note to the Reader

This book is written in British English except where fidelity to other languages or accents are appropriate. Some words and phrases may differ from US English.

ISBN: 9798485998721

CONTENTS

Final Solutions 7

Overture in Arcadia 15

The Drums of War 26

The Picture of Health 38

Physician Heal Thyself 52

Acts of War 62

Of Spiders and Flies 76

The Hunt 100

Clear Conscience 109

Secrets and Lies... 127

Who Was Doctor Satan? 139

About the Author... 146

More Books by Ryan Green... 149

Free True Crime Audiobook.. 153

Final Solutions

The streets of Paris were clotted with smog. Many months had passed since the occupation began, and the factories that had fallen silent as the French war effort ended had been brought lurching back to a semblance of life. Conscription orders had gone out; every able-bodied man was to report to their assigned duty or face repercussions. So those undead bastions of industry spewed forth new, bilious clouds that turned the sky and the streets black by midafternoon each day.

That conscription programme was how they had found the Doctor. There had always been whispers about him, even before the war. Insinuations that he was willing to do the things that his more ethical compatriots would not. Yet now in this dark time, there was no denying that his moral flexibility was just what France needed. He had no compunctions about lying to the Nazis. Whatever else he might have been, abortionist or drug peddler, there was no denying that he was at his heart a Frenchman, and the same longing for freedom from the yoke of tyrants burned in his heart. His were the people who had beheaded their kings – was it any wonder that the little Austrian with the funny moustache grated on his nerves?

So when the conscription notices were sent out from whatever dingy office the Germans had commandeered, a series of polite envelopes were returned with a signed notice from a medical professional that they must be excluded from any forced work programmes on the basis of disability. There were not many of these envelopes, not nearly enough to arouse any sort of suspicion, but it seemed that Paris housed many more disabled people than any census might have suggested.

In particular, those who resided by the Rue des Rosiers found that they were not required to attend any of these new jobs that the Nazis had found for them. Indeed the whole Jewish Quarter in Marais seemed to have suffered dreadful injuries during the Great War, and such being the case, only a very few of the men could be compelled to manufacture munitions and materiel for the war effort against the Allies. Very few Jewish men had to endure the judging eye of the Nazi overseers, quietly taking note of their heritage and preparing more permanent places for them and their families.

There were rumours about the Doctor even among those who made use of his services. There were those who said that he was more than just a kindly man, willing to sign what he must to protect his fellow Frenchmen from the wicked invader. Some whispered that he was a part of the underground resistance. Others that he served as a spy, feeding information out of France to the allies. It was this last part that was of interest to the Parisian Jews, because for information to get out, a route was required.

As the occupation marched on through the year with its jackboots shined, people began to go missing. There was no mystery whether the Nazis were responsible – if anything, they broadcasted the fact of their relocation programmes and ghettos with great delight, as though the fear and the cruelty was the point of the exercise. The missing people that interested the Jewish community were the ones who put all of their affairs in order, withdrew all of the money from their accounts, and then vanished without a trace.

The French police made no effort to find them. If anything, they made deliberate efforts to muddy the trail where they could. Meanwhile, the Gestapo were run off their feet chasing after all of the very real spies and saboteurs still at work in Paris. They had no time to be chasing ghosts. If some of the racial enemies of the German state vanished, then whoever was responsible was doing their work for them.

Yet the trail was followed. Not by the police, or the Fuhrer's errand boys, but by the Jewish community itself. None of them begrudged anyone their secrecy, but if there was a way out before the trap snapped shut, then of course they were going to take it.

Valentin was the latest to follow that trail. He had not been lucky enough to avoid Nazi attention. He knew that his name was on their lists, that it was just a matter of time before the knock came in the middle of the night and he was hauled off onto a train to nowhere, never to be seen or heard from again. He did not know about the camps, the gas, the final solution – none of that would become public knowledge until long after the war was done – but he knew that danger stalked him. Doom followed in his footsteps every day that he trudged to his factory work and the overseers peered down at him, noting the curls of his dark hair, his pronounced nose, and his surname staring up at them from their list. He had seen the little star beside his name in their record books. He could see that same star alongside rows that had been crossed through. Men, Jewish men, who were no longer expected to return to work in the factory. He was not going to let them do that to him. He was not going to become another line in another ledger, moved from column to column.

So he was here in the smog now, stalking from alleyway to alleyway, hoping that he would not be caught breaking curfew. It had been a simple enough piece of detective work for him to realize that every one of the people who had vanished had also received a writ from the Doctor excusing them from work. Once you knew about that one illicit endeavour of his, it seemed quite obvious that the Doctor's underground connections were getting the endangered out of Paris and into safer territory, sending his spying reports along in their hands to help the allies fight back against the occupation.

Every franc that Valentin owned was in his pockets. Whatever the cost to get out of France, he would pay it without complaint. What use was money if you were dead or imprisoned?

The same smog that made it easy to avoid the eyes of the patrolling Germans made the city into a stranger. Valentin had spent all of his years on these streets, and the Germans had made them alien to him. Not just their flags flapping in the breeze or the checkpoints they set up around the city – even the air tasted wrong. Where once he could lift his nose and know at once whether he was close to the patisseries of the Rue de Seine or catch a waft of perfume warning him he was near to Montmartre, now the whole city stank of relentless industry. He had to walk the streets by memory now, trusting his feet to carry him more than his eyes to lead him.

Yet despite all that had changed, memory still served him well. Though it may have been hours after the curfew, his journey through the city had been swift and unnoticed. He scrambled up the steps to the Doctor's door and rapped on it firmly with his knuckles, eyes darting around to make sure that he was not seen by any neighbour or potential Nazi collaborator. Just when he was beginning to wonder if he should knock again, harder, and risk drawing attention, the door popped open like a cork from a bottle of champagne and the Doctor was there in all his quiet dignity.

With just a glance, he made his diagnosis of Valentin's situation and swiftly ushered him inside. With the door closed behind them, he ushered him through, past the waiting room set up in what should have been a living room and into the doctor's office that had supplanted the house's kitchen. Even though it was quite apparent what his purpose in visiting was, still Valentin blurted out, "I must get out of France."

"I know. I know why you are here."

Even so, it seemed that there was an inevitability to their movements. The Doctor headed to his place behind the desk, Valentin to his place on the patient's side, awaiting the prognosis. "They have already marked me. I must escape."

It seemed enough to give the Doctor pause. He did not look startled, but he did pause in his digging through the desk drawers. "You have not led them here? You have not left any note or message of your plans that might be found? You have not spoken to others of your purpose in visiting me?"

"No. None of that." Valentin was aghast. "I'm no fool, Doctor. I would not bring trouble to your door."

The Doctor resumed his digging, emerging with medicine bottles and papers that had been hidden away inside of other folders. "Then you are wiser than many of the poor panicked souls that I have helped these past months."

With all the pieces of paper laid out before him, the Doctor seemed to remember what came next. He blinked. "Money. Do you have money? You will need it to start your new life in South America."

"South America?"

"Argentina. As far from the awful war as I can send you. Somewhere you and your kind can be safe at last. There are friends already waiting for you there, more of your own people than you can imagine."

"I... yes... I have money."

He fumbled in his pockets for it. He had expected to pay dearly to be smuggled out of Paris, but now it sounded as though he would be allowed to keep what wealth he managed to smuggle with him. He had foreseen dread and danger, a life of struggle once he was out of France, but from the way that the Doctor described it, it sounded almost like a holiday.

"Good, good. You have it with you? You are ready to depart?"

There was no turning back now. Valentin nodded. "Yes."

"Excellent." The Doctor clapped his hands together. "Most excellent. There are some preparations that we must make before I take you through the tunnel. There are health concerns that I must make you aware of. The viruses and bacteria in Bolivia are not the same as those here. You shall require vaccination to ensure your safety."

Valentin was confused but still went through the motions of stripping off his coat and rolling up his sleeve as the Doctor drew out syringes. "Bolivia?"

Once more the Doctor froze in place. Like he was a turning record that had stuttered out of its groove for a moment. "My pardon, I mean Argentina, of course. Many things on my mind. You must excuse me."

"Of course, Doctor. I cannot imagine all of the strain that you are under as a part of the resistance, and I cannot thank you enough for this. You cannot know how much the work that you do has meant to us."

Like he was reading from a script, the Doctor went through his motions, drawing medicine up from the bottle. "My work has always been well compensated. I have no need of your thanks."

"I do not mean your doctoring, sir. I mean the help that you give to my people. To all of France."

Without delay or warning, the Doctor crossed the distance and plunged the syringe into Valentin's arm. He let out a surprised yelp, but he did not jerk away. The Doctor stepped back and watched him. "I am a doctor. When there is pain, I seek to ease it. When there is sickness, I seek its cure. When there is a disease that I can remove from the world with just a simple injection, of course I will do it without question."

The pain in Valentin's arm had faded almost immediately, replaced with numbness that now spread out. His arm hung limp and useless, and as he tried to take in a breath to cry out and tell the doctor that something had gone wrong, his lungs stopped drawing in air. He tried to rise, to wave his arms, to do something, anything to alert the Doctor to his plight, but the man's back was turned. He was digging through the pockets in Valentin's jacket without a glance to his patient, behaving as though he were the only one in the room.

Valentin toppled from his chair, landing with a sickening crunch upon the tiled floor, then flopping helpless and hopeless upon the ground, his broken nose smeared blood in a curve towards the heels of the man who had killed him. For his part, the Doctor only looked down and tutted at the mess. All of Valentin's money and papers had been extracted with practised ease from the places where he had hidden them, the lining of his coat was slit open with a scalpel to retrieve those pieces he had hidden. The cold was across his chest now, down in his guts, climbing up his throat, It was competing with the burn of his stilled lungs to be felt in these final moments. His body was dead now, he knew that much at least, but still his eyes moved, his brain sparked. He was still there when the Doctor started stripping him. Marking the points where he would separate his limbs from his torso with a pen. Planning his disposal.

He was still alive right up until the moment that the Doctor fetched out his bone saw and crouched down on the tiled floor beside him and smiled for the very first time since he had met him – wide and leering and full of such horrifying delight that Valentin was glad that he would not be here to see what came next.

Overture in Arcadia

The Roman city of Auxerre was already well on its way to flourishing before anything resembling modern France was within imagination. It was always at the heart of the Burgundy region, and while other cities may have grown larger than it with time, it remained a powerhouse of industry and trade, thanks in no small part to the world-famous wine, which was produced there for millennia. It was in this bustling metropolis on the edge of the rolling vineyards that on January 17, 1897, Marcel Petiot was born.

His father, Felix Irénée Mustiole Petiot, was an employee of the French Postal Service for the town, and his mother, Marthe Marie Constance Joséphine Bourdon, was his wife of many years. Both of them delighted in the long-awaited arrival of their firstborn son, and he was lavished with all the luxury and attention that they could offer.

His early years passed without much of note occurring in his life. He was an intelligent and precocious child, quick to learn and quick to question those things that his parents took for granted. It was not difficult to foresee a successful future for him in those days.

He began to attend the local school, and while his brilliance could not be denied by his teachers, what really stood out was the disruptive influence that he brought to their classes. He had no respect for the authority of his teachers, talking over them and challenging them at every turn, until eventually his reputation was not that of a gifted student but of a troublesome one. Between the ages of six and ten, he was suspended from school on multiple occasions, often after week-long arguments with his teachers. Neither of his parents knew how to tame the boy. Neither discipline nor kindness seemed to make any difference to his fundamental character, and it was that character that drove his teachers to despair. For a time after each suspension, he would be quiet and obedient, but then something new would set him off.

The other children delighted in his antics, of course, and he was well regarded by his prepubescent peers as a result, but his actual relationships with them were strained by the same character flaws that made his parents worry about him and his teachers dread their encounters. It was less that he was domineering – a bully would have been a quite normal thing for a child of their age to endure – rather it was that he simply did not care about the thoughts and opinions of others. Whatever he wanted to do at any given moment was the only correct thing to do, and whatever he said was law as far as he was concerned. If it was disputed, then the one arguing with him could be ignored entirely, as they were simply wrong. All of which made it rather difficult to play with him.

Of course, there were plenty who were quite willing to go along with him in whatever he said or did, but even that introduced problems. He would comment that a thing should belong to him and expect those with him to either turn over their belongings or steal it for him, then they would face his contempt if they failed to make the world as he decreed it. Worse still, his precociousness had continued as he grew older – he read far beyond his level, spoke with those many years his senior as though they were his equals, and developed an unhealthy fixation upon things that were considered too mature for him.

At that grand old age of eleven, he isolated one of his female classmates and attempted to coerce her into having sex with him. She did not even understand what was being asked of her. Only that he was trying to remove her clothes and to touch her in places that she had been told strangers should not touch. A teacher discovered him in the act before it could go too far, and the school downplayed the danger involved to her parents when she went crying to them that night, explaining everything away as childish inquisitiveness about the bodies of others. Yet still, Marcel was suspended from school as though it were something far more sinister.

That he was suspended once more came as no surprise to his beleaguered parents. They assumed that the crisis point had been yet another argument with a teacher or squabble that he would not let go of. They did not note the looks that the teachers gave them when handing over their charge; they did not hear the rumours circulated about their son and about them as the creators of such a creature. They did not know of the scandal that was rippling out through their community, marring their family name. They knew nothing of any of it. Only that Marcel was home once more, sitting at the kitchen table and scowling out of the window when he should have been in his classes.

There were stern words spoken to the boy when he returned to school, but not coordinated ones. No single person of authority had been granted the fraught duty of explaining exactly what he had done wrong, or why it was considered so terrible. Most of them could not bring themselves to even describe what he had attempted, let alone tell him why it was unacceptable. Instead, he was bombarded with fragmentary rage on all sides. As though every one of the teachers in the school had now marked him as their enemy for no good reason at all.

His silence stretched out longer this time, not because he had been more chastened by his latest suspension, but because he still had not deciphered the situation and could not plan his next move accordingly. All that he knew truly was that he was under constant scrutiny and pressure in a way that he had never been before. His response to that pressure was explosive.

Before even a year was past, young Marcel was permanently expelled from his school. Not as a result of the accumulated rebellions that he had committed throughout his education, but for committing a single act that was so far beyond the pale that it was impossible to ignore or downplay.

Felix Petiot owned a pistol. A small revolver that he maintained carefully in full view of his son at the communal dining table. He had expressed to his son how dangerous the weapon was, that it was not a toy, that it was never to be touched, and that he was never to seek the place that it had been hidden. Everything in his demands had been sternly spoken, and so reasonable, that it was fair to think that the child would never even consider defying this edict. Any other child would not have. Yet in the heart of Marcel was a perpetual fire of rebellion. No matter how reasonable a prohibition might be, he felt compelled to buck it. No matter what consequences breaking the rules might have for him in the future, he could not comprehend those consequences as worse than the denial of his freedom in the present. He felt the oppressive weight of every rule like a physical strain, and each and every time he had the opportunity to lessen that load, he took it.

It was impossible to tell when he first acquired his father's gun, or for how long he had been roaming the city with it tucked away inside his school satchel. It could have been found and stolen on the very same day that he pulled it out in class and discharged it into the ceiling, or he could have been patiently bearing the weight of it for weeks or even months before that fateful day.

The strange thing was, there didn't seem to be any reason for him to have pulled out the gun and fired it. He was not involved in one of his usual arguments. He was not trying to get his way, or force someone else to obey him. It was as though he did it for no purpose other than to make the statement that he would not be ignored and he would not be controlled.

The expulsion was immediate, his father's wrath entirely predictable. He set so few limitations upon his son, knowing how little he liked him, yet the one thing that he had asked him to never do was the thing that he had chosen to do. Adding to the confusion was the boy's young age. He was still only eleven years old. Could a child of eleven even comprehend the significance of his actions? Certainly he was precocious and read philosophy and science texts meant for those many years his senior, but did he comprehend them on an emotional level as well as an intellectual one? Could he even be held responsible for the things that he had done?

It was, and remains, a grey area in the eyes of morality and the law. So his expulsion was the limit of the punishment that young Marcel received.

In the privacy of his own home, he continued his studies, with his mother serving as an interim schoolmistress, wise enough not to restrict him or make any demands on him beyond that which his own curiosity already did. It seemed that the safest and surest way to maintain his good behaviour was simply to keep him engaged in his studies, and before long both parents began to convince themselves that the troubles he had been experiencing in school were due to the lack of challenge that he faced. If he had been engaged by the work, surely he would not have become frustrated. If he had been absorbed in his studies, the way that they could see he was at home, then surely he would have had no time for any of the anti-social behaviour of which he had been accused.

They managed to convince themselves, yet again, that the problem was not in their son, but in the world outside of their home. And with that conviction half-formed in their hearts, they set out to put him back into that world once more.

What followed were a series of brief stays in educational institutions around the region. With Marcel's reputation for poor behaviour, he was generally accepted to them on the condition of unrelenting excellence, and the moment that his usual habits came out, he was ejected just as swiftly.

He passed out lewd photographs in one school. In the next, he propositioned a male student for sex in much the same way that he had the girl when he was eleven. When he met up with a friend from his early years in a third school, the duo decided to re-enact a circus performance that they fondly recalled, with the other boy placing himself against the classroom door as Marcel launched knives at him. Never striking, but always coming perilously close. He was quite offended to have been expelled from that school as he felt that he had not done anything wrong. If he had missed one of his throws, he could certainly have understood the furore that followed, but no damage was done except to the door.

It had been a simple enough matter for Felix and Marthe to ignore the worst excesses of their son's behaviour when he comprised their entire world, but with the birth of a second son, Maurice, their opinions on the matter began to change. Maurice was not brilliant in the way that their older boy was, but what he lacked in genius, he more than made up for in humanity. As he grew to school age himself, the stark contrast between him and his brother began to weigh on them.

Physicians were consulted about the boy on several occasions during those years. It seemed that in addition to his behavioural problems at school, some other concerning patterns had emerged in his home life. He was prone to convulsions and spasms in the evenings. Often, he would be found roaming around the house in the dead of night, sleepwalking. In addition, it seemed that there were issues with bladder control, resulting in wet beds and trousers. None of these things were ever observed outside of the family home in any account of his early life, and it is possible that these physicians later fabricated such stories to fit in with the predominant views on mental illness when Marcel's later actions came to light. Similarly, accounts have surfaced of young Marcel capturing and torturing animals to death, but there seems to have been no note or record of such things at the time, only many years later when he had become a public figure. It is entirely possible that he did such things, even likely, but there is no evidence attesting to these events that can be entirely trusted.

In 1912, a far greater tragedy struck the family. Marthe died suddenly in what bore the hallmarks of an early outbreak of the Spanish Flu. The whole family was bereft, of course, but Maurice was still young enough that the grief was tempered by a lack of understanding. Felix and Marcel understood what had happened all too well. The grief hung over them, dampening their spirits and tainting what little joy they could still find in life. When Felix sought out a new job so that he could leave the city where he had known love, it was of no surprise. He moved to Joigny, some 15 miles from Auxerre, took on a job in their postal office, and took a small apartment for himself. Marcel and Maurice were left behind in the care of their aunt.

The same grief that had made Felix take flight had left Marcel quiet and introverted for the first time in his life. His aunt had no trouble with him in the first few months of their cohabitation, and little Maurice was so lost and confused at his abrupt abandonment by both of his parents that he was probably the most troublesome to her, clinging desperately to the only adult that he still knew.

The intention was for the boys to finish out their school year then follow after their father once he had settled in the new town. But, of course, that was working off the dubious assumption that Marcel could make it through a school year without finding himself expelled once more. His grief kept him silent and sullen for a time, but it did not last forever, and his fury at being abandoned by both of his parents in so short a period of time soon came out in vicious flares of temper. Within a few months, he was expelled and, at a loss, his aunt sent the boy off to join his father in Joigny so that Maurice might still get the benefit of an education at least.

He did not receive a warm welcome. He was exiled there in disgrace, and his father made sure to let him know precisely how disappointed he was in his son. Previously, Marcel had taken such chiding in his stride, another statement made by someone who was simply wrong, but now he was already brimming with anger towards his father, and his attempts at discipline only swelled his burgeoning hatred.

While Felix tried to secure him a place in one of the local academies, hoping that word of his son's wickedness had not spread too far afield, Marcel set out to get petty revenge.

After only a few short months at an academy in Joigny, he was expelled for overexcitement and unruly behaviour, freeing up his days to pursue his new interest, shaming his father as thoroughly as possible in the eyes of his peers and neighbours. What had begun as a spate of petty thefts from local businesses soon escalated into something more objectionable to the law. His father had no shop that could be robbed, but there were post boxes dotted around Joigny, clearly marked with the postal service's livery. It was one of these that Marcel attacked next, breaking into the box, he made off with all of the letters inside.

A trail of discarded letters and envelopes formed a breadcrumb trail back to the apartment that they had taken on, and it was a simple matter for the police to track him down and place him under arrest for destruction of public property.

Until now, such matters as had arisen through the course of Marcel's petty criminal career had been dealt with through cash payments, apologies, and shaken hands. People knew his family, and they had heard tales of the troubles that the boy caused them and were, to an extent, sympathetic. The weight of community forced all into complicity with him. If they did not want to bring his family trouble, then it was a simple matter to approach his father and broach the subject of missing items at a later date. It was well known that the boy was not entirely normal and that holding him to the same standards as other children his age was unfair, yet now he had crossed a line that forced the involvement of the law, and it was well known that Lady Justice played no favourites.

Yet for all that it was unrelenting, there could be no argument that the legal system of France was not fair. Before young Marcel's case had even come close to a court, doctors were brought in to assess his mental state, and it was not difficult for them to note the many curiosities in the boy's behaviour, his history across so many schools that it was difficult to count, and even the relatively recent death of his mother. By March of 1914, one psychiatrist was ready to absolve him, stating that Marcel was "an abnormal youth suffering from personal and hereditary problems which limit to a large degree his responsibility for his acts."

A panel of doctors presented their evidence to the court, and by the time that Marcel himself was called to the chambers, the judge had already come to an informed decision upon the matter, declaring that "the accused appears to be mentally ill." The charges against him were dropped and he was passed into the care of his father once more. Felix had his other son settled nicely into a routine by the time that the wayward one came wandering back through his door. They were making a life for themselves in Joigny. It was not as sweet and comfortable as the one that they had clung to in Auxerre, but it was as good as they could make it, and he had no intention of letting Marcel's anger at him poison the little joys that they had managed to cultivate. A serious solution to the boy's behaviour was required, and professional intervention may well be required to provide it.

After a failed attempt to ship him off to a school in Dijon that had promising results with troubled students, he was placed in a specialist academy in Paris to complete his education. In an environment that was more prison than classroom, he found a new purpose in his studies, excelling across the board when it became apparent that graduation was the only way that he would ever be allowed to depart.

Proving without a doubt that his problems with schooling had been entirely behavioural, he graduated with the top marks in that particular academy, grades so high that he might have proceeded to higher education if he so wished. He did not wish to, of course. He had worked hard to earn his freedom from any institution, so of course he had no desire to commit himself to another immediately upon escape.

Of course, fate was not so kind as to allow him any measure of freedom for long. He had scarcely made it back to his father's home in Joigny before his draft letter came, and come January of 1916, he was shipped out with the French Infantry to face the German invasion from the West.

The Drums of War

France was ill-equipped for modern warfare. Her soldiers did not even have helmets until a month into the war, their munitions manufacturing could not come close to the requirements of a contemporary battlefield, and their artillery stood silent more often than it was fired upon the German interlopers. The Alsace line was held thanks to the fortifications that had been constructed there in the wake of the Franco-Prussian war and the pure grit of the French soldiers upon the ground. It did not help that their command was still living in a past century, anticipating glorious cavalry charges and hand-to-hand combat in place of the trenches, gas, and explosives that became necessary just to hold the line. The surprise invasion through Belgium almost broke the French defences entirely. The German war machine rolled across the undefended border of that third party and into French territory before troops could even be deployed, and among those who were hauled off of the front lines and rapidly deployed by rail on the unexpected front with little to no support, planning, or orders was Marcel Petiot.

The department of Aisne was one of the few places where geography might present some advantage to the defenders. Three great rivers crossed and intersected it, and while there was no time to destroy bridges ahead of the German arrival, they still provided choke points, preventing the invader from bringing the full brunt of its superior numbers to bear.

Up until this point in the war, Marcel had acquitted himself well. While he was not well-liked by his fellow soldiers, there could be no denying that he was effective in the field – He was a solid shot, and more than willing to take the fight to the enemy with little to no fear for his safety. Fixing bayonets and leaping over the top of a trench to charge towards enemy gun emplacements required something beyond courage, something more closely resembling madness, and that was Marcel's greatest virtue in those bloody days.

In Aisne, where it seemed that there was no hope of meaningful victory, he became the rock on which his unit clung against the rising tides of history – spite and determination wrapped up in fierce, almost psychotic, hatred of the Germans trying to stroll in and steal the hard-won freedom of France. There was the usual bravado among soldiers on the train to deployment, talking of how they would fight to the last man to hold their land against the foreign aggressor, but there was truly no question in the minds of his comrades that if Marcel were literally the last Frenchman alive, he would still be out in the mud of Aisne fighting for every inch of it.

Which is why it was such a blow to his unit and the defenders in general when he was struck by shrapnel from one of the

German stick-grenades early in the opening of trench warfare. He had worked like the devil to dig in the earthworks that would be required to hold back the invaders, taking no rest or respite, and now just when the time came to defend them, he was struck down. Yet even then he could not countenance retreat. He accepted such field medicine as could be provided to him but insisted on fighting on even as everyone around him demanded that he head back behind the lines to seek proper treatment. He would not hear of it, dragging himself up to lean upon the side of the trench so that he might have a clear shot at the enemy.

He fought on for a time, making the Germans pay in blood for each step that they took onto French soil, but through it all, he was watering that same soil with his own life blood. His aim never wavered, but his motions became sluggish as his vision narrowed down to a dark tunnel with his rifle at one end and the enemy at the other. He did not even hear when the artillery began raining down death upon the French position. He did not flinch or hesitate as concussion after concussion rolled over him. His compatriots saw this and found their own courage, fighting on to the bitter end as the Germans' inexorable advance stuttered and slowed to a crawl.

They had done the impossible. The unstoppable German advance had been halted. They were no longer even attempting to advance on French positions. It was incredible to see. Yet still Marcel did not stop. He took shot after shot into the stilled German beast as the enemy milled about seeking cover. If this was his opportunity to thin their numbers, then he was going to take that opportunity.

When the gas was released, the French soldiers knew what it was. From the very beginning of the war, there had been talk among the officers about the use of gas by the Germans to clear advance positions, but the knowledge of it had not trickled down to the front lines until later, and this was in no small part deliberate. The idea that the enemy could turn the very air to poison was a debilitating one for morale. This was coupled with the fact that French materiel production was so slow that actually issuing gas masks to the soldiers on the front lines was a long way off.

By this point in the war, a mask was a part of every soldier's kit, and the tell-tale green-yellow clouds that were unleashed from canisters opened up on the battlefield were so well known that warning cries were scarcely even required anymore. With mechanical ease born of entirely too much practice, every soldier noted the situation and masked up.

All of them except for Marcel, of course. He had no awareness of anything going on around him in the haze of blood loss. He breathed the chlorine gas in deep.

When he awoke once more, he was in a field hospital almost an entire department away from the battlefield where he fell. Every breath was agony. The shrapnel that they could not dig out of him before stitching him shut shifted and ground against his bones when he tried to move. More painful than all of that was the knowledge that came later, that after he had been rendered unconscious, the Germans had charged across the gas-shrouded battlefield and taken the position that he had done his damnedest to lie down and die for.

The war raged on far beyond the walls of his hospital room, and Marcel longed for it with every inch of his being. Yet now that he was no longer in the field, the doctors were taking a rather intense interest in him. Things that had been ignored because it was so vital to have soldiers in the field seemed less important to the people tasked with ensuring the survival of humanity through the conflict. To his doctors' eyes, it seemed that Marcel's manias and obsessions were symptomatic of shellshock. That his desire to throw himself back into the field so soon after his injuries, even before they had fully healed, was likely part of a self-destructive pattern of behaviour that they had observed in some of the men who had lost their reason to the rattle of shells.

Marcel's injuries healed and his lungs returned to working order in time, but still, he was not released. Rather, he was transferred yet farther from the front lines to take some rest at a hospital in Orleans, where they hoped that he might regain some measure of calm and composure, or at least be kept from endangering others with the reckless streak that they assumed had developed as a result of his injuries. They could not know that the man was already profoundly damaged before he had even taken to the field of battle. Or that a madman in the mad world of trench warfare appeared to be the sanest of them all.

Deprived of a target for all of his nervous energies, it did not take long before Marcel's condition began to deteriorate. Boredom had always been his nemesis, and in the various rest homes that the medical establishment shuffled him to, it stalked his every waking hour. There were no books for him to read, no battles for him to plan. All that was left to amuse him was the petty mischief that he had filled his days with in between expulsions from school.

There were no official complaints about his attempting to seduce members of staff or other patients in the rest homes, but this is most likely because records of such things were not kept, rather than because he had suddenly become chaste upon reaching maturity. His crimes remained as petty as they had ever been, stealing blankets and hoarding them in his room before beginning to collect other army supplies in the same hoard. Morphine was the drug of choice in those rest homes, and it was not long before Marcel had acquired a syringe and a steady supply of the drug to take the edge off his boredom. What had started as a hobby to fill his long empty days soon blossomed into a full-on narcotic addiction, and as the chemicals blossomed through his body, ridding him of all worries, so too fled the last measures of restraint that he had put upon himself.

Wallets began to go missing, both from patients and staff. Watches and cufflinks, too – small, easily palmed items that could be resold for no small value on the black market. There was always a degree of theft expected of soldiers, so this too drew little attention, but then the kleptomania took a turn for the bizarre. The things being stolen were no longer items of material value, but things of personal value. Photographs of sweethearts back home. Letters from worried family members. It was as though Marcel was trying to steal a whole life for himself outside of the confines of the hospital. To pretend that the lives of the other soldiers belonged to him, and that he had friends and family waiting for him at the far side of all this misery.

These thefts were too obviously the symptom of a more serious mental issue for the staff to ignore, and after the building was searched and his little hoard uncovered, once more the implacable engines of justice were forced to swing into action. Stealing military materiel during the war was an extremely serious crime for which others had suffered summary execution. Marcel's circumstances prompted the judge to mercy, as it seemed apparent that his actions were the result of some compulsion rather than a deliberate attempt to sabotage the war effort, but even so, there was a minimum custodial sentence attached to them.

From the rest home, he was moved to the Orleans jail. It was not his first time in confinement, and he adapted swiftly to his new surroundings, but once again his loss of freedom seemed to enrage him. He did what he must to get through his imprisonment, but all of the exaggeration of his neuroses that had occurred when he was left entirely to his own devices came to an abrupt halt.

After his sentence was served out, he was brought back before a tribunal to judge not whether he was fit to be returned to society, but whether he could be redeployed to the front lines. The war had not been going well in the intervening months while Marcel was gone, and while there was little doubt among those called to judge that the man had psychological problems, they seemed much less of a pressing issue now than when he had first been sent off for respite.

Those who had known Marcel during his first tour of duty had expected him to come roaring back into the fight, ready to take the war to the Germans, but his entire attitude to the war seemed to have changed by the time that he was redeployed on the front lines. Just as he felt that his father had betrayed him in his youth when all of his efforts had been devoted to making his father proud, now he felt that France had betrayed him as he tried diligently to serve her. Or at least the military establishment, which he now saw as no different from his captors during his time in jail and respite. He followed orders haltingly when he was in view of officers, but otherwise disregarded them. He would follow his own best judgement in the field, often leading to him butting heads with those who outranked him, but never quite crossing the line into open enough insubordination that he might be returned to civilian life.

He saw combat again before much time had passed, and he acquitted himself just as well as any one of his peers, but the patriotic fury that had driven him in the early days of the war seemed to have vanished entirely, and his actions became, if not cowardly, then at least sane enough for self-preservation to be the dominant drive.

Without the blinkers of his obsession, it soon became apparent to him that time on the front lines was essentially a death sentence, as one by one the members of his unit were plucked from beside him by artillery fire and stray shots. If he remained in the trenches, he was certain that he was going to die, and he refused. He refused to lie down and die for a country that had cast him aside so cruelly.

There was no fear of pain in him, not after those agonizing months following his breathing of chlorine gas, but there was now a fear of oblivion. And if all that it took to ensure his survival was a little more pain, then he was willing to suffer it and inflict it as required.

It was a simple thing to move along the jagged bayonet wound in the landscape until the soldiers around him thinned and the trench began to shallow out. Close enough that a scream could still be heard, but far enough away from the judging eyes of officers and those children they had stuffed into the uniforms of men that he could do as he pleased without risk of discovery.

He set his rifle down with care and lay back with his shoulders pressing into the soft sod behind him. There were no boards to hold back the troubled earth here. If a shell went awry and the trench fell, then it fell.

This was the mentality that Marcel was seeking, the devil-may-care attitude that would allow him to pass through this fresh trial and on to safety. In the distance, he could hear the German guns rattling, the whine of artillery soaring through the air to bring death raining down. The land around him was no longer the France that he knew but a cratered mess of mud and bloodshed and fear that made not a jot of sense to even his troubled mind.

He drew his pistol and took aim. Never in all of his service had he flinched away from pulling the trigger, from taking the shot that would kill a man or save his own life. He had none of the moral compunctions that made his countrymen easy prey to the German jackals. He was willing to fire. Always willing to fire. Yet here he lay, pistol pointed, his muddy boot there in the iron-sights. Just a squeeze of the trigger and he would be gone, back behind the lines to some comfortable hospital where he could ride out the final days of the war in comfort and a morphine-induced haze. He would not have to worry about rats chewing at his fingers while he slept, about the stray shot making its way through the soil to leave him dead without warning, about the stern-faced aristocratic officers who looked at him and the other enlisted as little more than pawns in some great game. Numbers to be shuffled around their sheets.

With one last ragged breath, he steadied the shaking of his arm and fired his pistol into his foot.

The pain was not immediate. Instead, a sudden shock of cold enveloped the place where he could already see blood bubbling up. That same grey haze that had swallowed up the world when he'd been injured before washed in, and things stopped making sense. He had a gun in his hand, but he would not be needing that anymore, so he flung it away. He was injured, so the rest of his troop should come running to help him. Last time it had been a struggle to stop them – why wasn't anyone coming to take him away from all this? He was bleeding. He could see light through the other side of his foot. Where was his help? His respite?

He lay there bleeding for long moments as the pain started up before he realised his mistake. He was not screaming or shouting, the way that those children dressed as men did each time they were injured. It did not come naturally to him, to admit to pain or loss or defeat. He had to force himself to shout out, and even then his unpopularity among the other men made them in no rush to come dawdling along and see to his needs.

Eventually they came, and he was stretchered out of the trenches, passing by those scowling officers who knew very well what he had just done to shirk his duty but could not prove it. Officially it was an accidental misfire, of the sort that happened all too often among the barely trained soldiers who now manned the trenches, but both soldiery and doctors knew a deliberately self-inflicted wound, placed where it would disable but put the victim in no actual danger. Communist seditionists had spread pamphlets among the soldiers instructing them on just how to inflict such injuries upon themselves, alongside the more pro-active demands for the working class to rise up against those leaders who were willingly feeding them into the meat grinder of trench warfare. Regardless of the cause of the injury, he was first placed in a field hospital to receive some hasty treatment, then passed back out of the warzone to another rest home where he might recover. To his surprise, once the wound in his foot had healed up, he did not have to face another panel for psychological evaluation. Rather, he was attached immediately to a new unit and deployed to the front once more.

His behaviour this time around made his haphazard approach to soldiery during his last deployment look angelic by comparison. He ignored all orders, did as he pleased, and laughed in the face of anyone who challenged him. At the Dijon railroad depot, he displayed violent convulsions and ended up lying unconscious by the side of the rails for most of the day before his unit retrieved him and loaded him into the train beside them for their return to the front.

Headaches plagued him, and he spent as much time under observation in the field hospital as he did in the trenches. While there, the doctors observed a swath of new symptoms that had recently been associated with shellshock. Amnesia, suicidal tendencies, sleepwalking, and depression were added to the spate of other conditions already listed on his chart.

The officers he had been assigned to saw him as a danger to the safety of those around him and diligently filed to have him discharged from the army on a disability pension, as so many of the shellshocked had been. He was barely back in the field for three weeks before his long-standing history of mental illness caught up to those administrators who had redeployed him to begin with and they issued his 40-percent disability pension and discharge notice with all haste.

Military police came to collect him from his emplacement, and he was smiling wildly to all of his comrades in arms as he abandoned them and headed back to the safety and security of civilisation. They thought that he was being carted off to jail for his refusal to do his duty. They thought that he was being punished. Instead, he was off to receive a steady income and all of the benefits of having been a war hero without ever having to put himself at risk again. Even the officers sent out to fetch him looked disgusted by the time that they had dropped him off at the train station.

The Picture of Health

With the war over, the people of France turned their attentions to those brave men who had fought for their freedom and returned home in tatters. The disability pension that Marcel received was not enough to support him, and he spent several months living in a state of destitution before a crusading lawyer applied for his pension to be increased to 100-percent as it had been for many of those who had been truly rendered incapable of functioning in society by the wounds that they had suffered in the war. Marcel was taken back into medical care so that he could be re-assessed, and it was not long before the doctors strongly advised in favour of the full pension. The author of the report also strongly suggested that Marcel be committed to an asylum for the insane until that pension was no longer required, but given the conditions of such places, the crusader who had gone out of his way to see the poorly veteran assisted chose not to repeat that information to the judge.

As it turned out, Marcel was already voluntarily in a mental hospital, not as a patient, but as an intern. Aided by an accelerated education programme for veterans, he undertook the study of medicine with the kind of passion that would have seemed alien to those who had known him in the war. A passion that would have been intimately familiar to his mother, were she still alive. His obsession with learning had returned at full power, and that manic energy drove him above and beyond the limits of his fellow students. In a mere eight months, he had completed medical school before launching into a two-year psychiatric internship at Evreux, which he served out with distinction.

In a small part, his desire to be a doctor was tied to his desire for ready access to morphine and the other narcotics that he had become addicted to during his hospital stays during the war, but in a far larger way, it was driven by his desire to take the place of the doctors. The ones who had decided his fate, time and again. He had always resented others having power over him, and now he had found a way to turn the tables, to become the one who made the life and death decisions that others would simply have to live with. The fact that the job came with wealth and status was secondary to the emotional surge that such rulership over his fellow man could grant him. On December 15, 1921, he received his full medical degree from the Faculté de Médeceine de Paris and was granted free rein to practise medicine anywhere in France. While he continued his service in Evreux for a brief while, he found that the modest living and strictly structured days of a facility doctor did not appeal to him in the long term, and he soon set out to create a practice for himself, where he was answerable to only himself, and where he might turn the practice of medicine into a profitable enterprise rather than just a means to preserve the lives of his fellow man, for whom he felt little. He reconnected with his brother Maurice during this time, visiting him and his wife in Auxerre, bragging of his exploits during the war, which Maurice had almost entirely avoided thanks to his age, and aggrandizing himself in stories, brandishing his medical degree as evidence of all that he had made of himself once he was out from under the oppression of their father.

It seems likely that his words might have been granted a little more credibility if he had not attempted to pocket the silverware at the dinner table. He would continue to ignore his father's attempts at contact and visit with his brother in the years to follow, though he was always forced to turn out his pockets after each visit to ensure that he had limited his pilfering to things that Maurice and his wife did not mind parting with.

The truth was, with his disability pension, Marcel did not need to work, let alone steal from his own family, but he had acquired a new mania in the intervening years, his kleptomania taken to its natural conclusion in a desire to hoard wealth so that he was no longer reliant upon anyone for anything.

He chose to establish his medical practice in the town of Villeneuve-sur-Yonne, an ancient village on the Yonne River, just a 40-kilometre drive from his childhood home of Auxerre and the brother that he had left behind there.

With his foot in the figurative door, Marcel took a moment to study his competition within the town: two established medical practices that had been tending to the community for decades without a single complaint. Then he formulated an attack upon them that was rooted in enough truth that it was impossible to deny. While he was only twenty-five years old and fresh from his training, the other doctors in Villeneuve-sur-Yonne were octogenarians. He printed fliers advertising his newly opened surgery.

"Dr Petiot is young, and only a young doctor can keep up to date on the latest methods born of a progress which marches with giant strides. This is why intelligent patients have confidence in him."

Business was soon booming, but Marcel had a level of financial success that seemed grossly disproportionate to the number of patients coming through his door. This was due partially to his willingness to prescribe addictive narcotics to anyone who desired them, constantly hiking up the price of the drugs until he had driven many of the addicts who approached him to the verge of bankruptcy. He also did a roaring trade in illegal procedures, such as abortions, which he could not advertise or officially discuss but could easily charge a small fortune for, with the implication that the excess money being spent would buy his silence and complicity. There were some accusations to this end by his fellow doctors in Villeneuve-Sur-Yonne, but it was quite simple for him to pass them off as jealous competitors rather than genuinely concerned professionals. He had always been less than cordial with them, given his aggressive advertising strategy, so it was hardly surprising that they weren't all that fond of him.

The doctors, of course, sought out some of his patients to testify against Petiot and see his license to practice medicine revoked, but as grim as any punishment that Marcel might have suffered would have been, the penalty for those seeking abortions was incarceration, and the addicts would have been left entirely without the vital source of their narcotics. Although he preyed upon the vulnerable, he was still more of an ally to them than the establishment, and whether they cared for him or not, they still could not go against him.

The real genius of Marcel's finances did not come from drug dealing or illegal abortions, however. Rather, it came from a very simple piece of fraud. For every appointment, procedure, and prescription, he charged his patients as was his right, but he also had them sign forms that they considered to be a normal part of a doctor's visit. These were applications for state funding to cover their treatment. For every little bit of work that Marcel did, he was paid twice. Once by the government medical assistance fund, established to help people in the wake of the war, and once by the patients themselves.

With such wealth gathered, it did not take long for the young and charming Doctor Petiot to begin attracting romantic prospects. He had no experience with romance prior to his arrival, given his rather unsavoury reputation when he was younger and the lack of women on the front lines of the war. To his surprise, he found himself to be quite competent at wooing. He spent quality time with many of the young bachelorettes of the town, telling every one of them whatever it was that they wanted to hear at any given moment. As it turned out, having no sense of morality or desire to pursue a relationship beyond reaching the point of carnal consummation made it much easier for him to deal with the opposite sex.

For the most part, shame kept his victims in this latest fraud from speaking out. After all, whatever damage might have been done to his reputation was minuscule compared to the harm that such an admission might make to a young lady hoping to make a good match. The fact that he was readily available to provide abortions to any woman who had the misfortune of falling pregnant made him even more appealing to a certain type of woman, but they were sadly not the ones that he pursued. Certainly, he would take his pleasure with any one of the addicts who could not cover the full cost of the drugs that he was offering them, but that did not mean he actively pursued them.

Rather, his interest was always in the young women in the town who were actively seeking marriage and family. Sometimes he found that he could stretch these affairs out over weeks or months before the woman discovered that he was being deceptive and entertaining others. In May of 1926, one of the women that he had successfully convinced that he would someday be wedding was the daughter of one of his elderly patients, a young lady by the name of Louise Delaveau. When she discovered that the man she'd given herself freely to had been lying to her all along, she did not wilt and sink into the background as his previous victims had. She was not afraid of hurting her reputation – she was too furious to even consider the possibility that she might bring harm to herself. Yet she did not travel the town screaming and damning his name when the truth came out. Instead, she went straight to the source of all her suffering in a rage.

Louise stormed into his home and practice, hands clenched into fists and rage burning within her. That was the last time that she was ever seen. She vanished without a trace.

Several days later, when her father still could not find her, the police became involved. They interviewed Marcel, who was quite candid about the courtship that he had been engaged in with young Louise. He claimed that he had not seen her either, and with his being a gentleman of good standing in the community, they were quite happy to take him at his word.

Still, they were not entirely incompetent in their investigation. Interviews with neighbours of Petiot recounted a story of his struggling to load a heavy trunk into his car on the night in question after the practice had been closed. He had struggled and cursed trying to load it in yet accepted no help when it was offered. His car was back the next morning, and there was no trace of the chest nor any indication of where he had gone with it.

Louise's disappearance was written off by the police as if she were a runaway. Her father never believed it, but her tempestuous nature had been the subject of discussion about town. Her flights of fancy and her temper were well known.

Throughout all of this, no small part of Marcel's money was being spent on medical supplies greatly more than the town's requirements. Some of it he meant to sell along to his addicts, others he intended to ship abroad to foreign powers that were still in a state of strife after the war and thereby to turn a profit, yet no small amount of the addictive narcotics he purchased were consumed on-site. The drug abuse that Marcel had undertaken when he was trapped in a rest home throughout most of the war had returned in full force now that he had ready access to his poison of choice. The medicine seemed to smooth out Marcel's rough edges, making him more palatable to the people of Villeneuve-sur-Yonne, who might have initially held some doubts about their new doctor. That smoothness would prove to be essential later in the year 1926, when Marcel decided to make the transition from private practice to public speaking. It seemed that the role of mayor had been vacated, and an election was to take place, an election that Marcel intended to win. It was not enough for him to be a respected professional and a pillar of the community. Now that he had greatness in his sights, he would not settle for anything less. His father had been nothing but a postal worker, and he was already so much more. How sweet it would be for the old man to learn of his son, the mayor of a whole town, surpassing him in every imaginable way. For a child who had been singularly unpopular among adults because of his behaviour, to be elected by those same people would be the ultimate vindication.

Of course, for all that he practised his speeches and wrote out policies to appeal to the lowest common denominator, Marcel still would not settle for any possibility of defeat. He had learned his lesson well from his medical practice, where he doubled his money each time with just a little bit of fraud. Now he meant to double his chances. Actual election interference was a little beyond his skill set, but Marcel did have plans in motion to ensure that he would be the winner.

When the time came for the public debate with his only opponent for the role, the other man found himself on the receiving end of a torrent of abuse from the crowd. Every time he attempted to answer one of Marcel's grandiose statements, he found himself drowned out in screams and insults. At one point, rotten fruit was even flung. It seemed obvious to the whole crowd that Marcel Petiot was the natural choice, when this other man couldn't even get out a sentence without enraging somebody. First he won the debate, then the election. Then, he found his accomplice in the crowd and paid him well for his time, his efforts, and his discretion.

Once he was the mayor, Marcel felt that he should be satisfied. He had surpassed anyone's wildest dreams for him. He had proven everyone who looked down on him wrong. He was the king of his tiny domain. So why did he still feel the same deep-seated discomfort in his spirit that had always been there?

He turned to those few men whom he considered friends to question his lack of contentment, and they were quick with the platitudes and suggestions to improve his lot in life. To them, his life probably seemed empty because he spent it alone. He needed to settle down now that he was a grown man with a grown man's position. A wife and children were sure to set him right in a way that his torrid affairs never had. They would give him stability and a mirror to hold up to his happiness.

With no better plan, he conceded to their suggestions and allowed them to begin reaching out through the expansive networks of their wives to find him a match. By spring of the next year, he had found the woman he meant to spend the rest of his life with, and they were engaged. Georgette Lablais was married to the mayor in 1927 and bore their son Gerhardt the following year.

It seems that matrimonial bliss had done nothing to settle the wilder parts of Marcel's nature. He remained the same man that he had been before the wedding, albeit now proceeding with a degree more care so that his attempted affairs with the young women of the town did not become public knowledge. Whatever he had hoped he would feel when he looked down upon his son simply was not there. He played the role of loving husband and father to the best of his considerable abilities, but something was missing from his heart that no amount of faking could ever entirely conceal.

At about this time in the young mayor's life, his past came back to haunt him. His disability pension was up for review, and it was requested that he be observed by a panel of psychiatrists to ensure that he was still sufficiently insane to be in receipt of the full amount. He responded with a scathing letter, decrying these observations as "exhibitionism" and informing the government that he would rather his payments stop than have to endure such an experience ever again. The checks continued to arrive. It seemed that his soldier's pride had touched the soft heart of someone in the disability pensions office.

At about the same time, a trunk was discovered in a nearby river. It contained the decaying and dismembered body of a young woman. She could not be identified due to the state of the remains, and the police made no connection to the disappearance of Louise Delaveau, but, of course, as the mayor of the nearest town, Marcel was informed of the discovery. He showed no sign of recognition.

Throughout all of this, he had continued lining his pockets at every opportunity, and as the mayor of a town, he now had access to a whole new scale of fraud. He took bribes and made arrangements for the town to suit his own business dealings, and when he couldn't take money directly from his constituents, he began to embezzle from governmental funds instead. Between those many shady financial deals and the outright theft of funds and property, it was not long before complaints about him began to flood into the local prefect's office.

In March 1930, a dreadful fire reduced the home of Armand Debauve to ashes while he was at work overnight in the local dairy. It would not be until morning that the fire could be brought down enough that any hint of what had happened before the blaze spread could be deciphered. Henrietta Debauve, Armand's wife, was found at the very centre of the fire, body blackened by the heat but signs of trauma still showing despite that. She had been beaten to death with a blunt instrument before arson was committed to cover up the murder. The police were immediately involved and suspected that Henrietta had interrupted a robber as he went about his business, given the small fortune of 20,000 Francs in cash that had been taken before the place was ignited.

Footprints were discovered in the dawn's light that led away from the house, through the fields, and back to the town of Villeneuve-sur-Yonne.

It was clear that their murderer lived in the nearby town, but his trail went cold once he was out of the muddy fields. As mayor of the town, Marcel, of course, put himself at the centre of the investigation, offering any help that could be mustered to the local police and even clumsily petting the bloodhounds that had been gathered to hunt down their killer. They had no luck tracking the killer's scent, looping endlessly back to the police and Marcel as they paraded through town.

There was a single witness to the Debauve murder: a Monsieur Fiscot, who had seen a dark-haired man coming and going frequently from the house in the prior months. A well-heeled man whom Fiscot suspected kept Henrietta Debauve as his mistress. Rumours about this affair had been circulating for weeks among the neighbours, with the odd hint having been dropped by Henrietta herself to her friends that she had taken a lover since her husband was so often absent due to his work as a union man in the dairies. Her story was that her lover was an important man in the local area. The kind of man who would lose all the respect of the community if a story of his infidelity came out. She found it romantic that he was so overcome by lust for her that he would risk it all.

Monsieur Fiscot was the lynchpin on which this story hung, but he was not a well man, plagued since middle age by rheumatoid arthritis. He was scheduled to come to the police station in Villeneuve-sur-Yonne to make his official statement the next day, and if it had been presented to the local police, the likelihood is that it would have given the rumours connecting their very own Mayor Petiot to the crime the credence required for them to investigate him.

As he had to make the trip into town anyway, he decided to visit the doctor for his medication. He was not shy about sharing his story with Doctor Petiot's secretary or any of the other people in the waiting room, feeling almost giddy with excitement to be involved in something so dramatic.

In the official records of the day, he stepped through into the doctor's office, explained his health concerns, and then left after only conversation. A few hours later he was struck down by an inexplicable aneurism, and as his personal doctor, Marcel was called out to determine with certainty that this was the cause of death. Less than three hours later, the death certificate was signed and filed at the police station where Fiscot had been headed.

In reality, things were not quite so simple. Marcel had heard all the things that Monsieur Fiscot had to say and had absolutely no intention of allowing him to say them in any official setting. The two of them struck up a conversation about new potential treatments for Fiscot's arthritis, and with the promise of near-miraculous improvements, he consented to receive an injection. The lethal overdose would not take effect until he was back out on the street, ensuring that no suspicion would fall upon the doctor's surgery for any sort of malpractice. The police investigation crumbled into abject failure in the weeks that followed. They knew nothing about the perpetrator other than that he now had a substantial amount of money and he lived in Villeneuve-sur-Yonne, but there had been no indication that any of the local lowlifes had suddenly come into good fortune. To the police, and everyone of note in the town, it was obvious that the rumours of Henrietta Debauve being the mayor's mistress were the same unfounded allegations that had been plaguing him since his very first day in office. To begin with, it seemed to be mere animosity on the part of the local man he had beaten at the polls. Stories about Marcel having lied about his health to escape service during the war were patently untrue, but now it seemed that any bad thing that happened in the town was somehow the direct consequence of the mayor's actions. When oil was stolen from the railyard, it was somehow Marcel who had committed the crime, even though he would have been stealing for no reason at all. Likewise, whenever a piece of paperwork was misfiled or funds held up in the town hall, it was somehow Marcel Petiot's work. The police would not have been surprised if some quarters of the town accused their mayor of starting the Great War if they thought that they could concoct some evidence for it.

By August of 1931, the many attempts to censure Marcel through normal political means had proven useless, and it became necessary for him to be suspended as mayor. It was a scandal throughout the whole province, but the political theatre that followed ensured that it would never be forgotten.

The entire village council resigned in solidarity with their beloved mayor.

The prefect's decision handed down from on high and passing hand to hand through the governmental bureaucracy had been almost entirely invisible to the common folk of the Yonne district. The outcry that followed – as the many people over whom his illegal dealings had provided blackmail material leapt to his defence – went beyond visible and into the realms of urban legend. Between the council's resignation, the obfuscating nature of the governmental processes that had led to his removal, and the frankly ridiculous amount of goodwill he had built up with the local people, he stepped up the ladder once more, transmuting infamy into fame and his defeat into a victory. Five weeks after his resignation from the mayor's role, he was elected as a councillor for the whole province.

Once more his reign was marred by allegations against him, culminating in his losing his seat on the council in 1932, after he was accused of stealing electrical supply for his private home by redirecting a wire from the town of Villeneuve-sur-Yonne, in a bizarre kind of revenge against the town that he felt had slighted him.

Of course, the loss of his seat meant very little to Marcel by this point as he had long since moved on, leaving behind an empty house lit up with stolen electricity, a cavalcade of complaints filed against him, and no forwarding address.

Physician Heal Thyself

Marcel had gathered up all of his substantial wealth and relocated his family to a new house and practice at 66 Rue Caumartin, in the 9th arrondissement of Paris. The residence had previously been home to the famous actor and bon vivant Edouard de Max. It was an ideal location for the kind of flamboyant persona that Marcel liked to project – the street was already a centre of public attention thanks to the proximity of the theatre – so when he put up his little billboard, announcing his services as a doctor of great renown, the evening crowds spread along the street would pass his signage on their way to a grand night out, and it was difficult for anyone to deny how impressive it all appeared to be. Despite his youth, Marcel proudly announced both his private practice in the Yonne district and several impressive internships at prestigious institutions around France. Places that he spoke of as fondly and easily as anywhere he had ever been in his life despite never having undertaken any of his studies there.

As a matter of fact, he had made a few slight typographical errors in his favour when writing up the sign. He had misspelt interné as interne, changing the meaning of the word from "a patient confined to the hospital" to "a student doctor attending there." He had been in every one of the institutes mentioned on his sign at some point during his life, either during the war or before, when his father still had hope that the sickness that had taken root in his son's mind might one day be cured. It made for a very impressive resume, and he soon began to draw in clientele from all walks of life across Paris. At first, only those who worked in the theatre and related industries would come to visit him for their ailments, but when it became clear just how free and easy he was with his prescription pad, and how willing he was to rid people of the awkward little problems that could sometimes make a young actress's career crumble, he was soon the subject of a great deal of word-of-mouth advertising that put his ridiculous billboard to shame.

As time went on, he replaced the original board with a brass plaque so crammed with endorsements that it was scarcely possible to judge their veracity. Many of these supposed quotes from patients ascribed him such miraculous healing powers as to be almost comedic. The local doctors did not find his behaviour to be a source of amusement, however. It did not take long before they filed an official complaint about his advertisement and the level of deception he committed with it. The plaque was ordered to be removed by the Paris Medical Association, but by then the damage had already been done. Marcel was the most popular doctor in the 9th.

As the years rolled on, Marcel's reputation only grew more and more celebrated. The people to whom he provided abortions and narcotics spoke of him even more highly than those to whom he provided more sanctioned care, hoping to curry the good doctor's favour, as it was known that he could be convinced to offer procedures and "cures" to those he considered friends. Despite regular complaints about his activities from the other doctors of Paris, not a single charge could be made to stick, and later interviews with over two thousand individual patients who had at some point been in his care produced not one unhappy customer.

In 1934, a thirty-year-old woman named Raymonde Hanss visited Petiot for a simple surgical procedure to drain an abscess in her mouth. He plied her with morphine until she fell unconscious, and only then did he remove his payment along with all other money from her purse, swiftly puncture the abscess with a brutal efficiency that would have been familiar to his companions on the battlefield, and then return to his ongoing medical studies as if she were not there at all.

As time rolled on, it became increasingly clear that Hanss was not going to wake up on her own. Marcel gave her a few slaps to see if he might rouse her, then when even that was unsuccessful, his patience came to its end. Hauling her out into the street and tossing her into the backseat of his car, he drove her home, let himself in and dumped her onto her bed where she could recover in peace without being any more of a nuisance to him. She never woke up.

It would be the next morning before Hanss's mother, Madame Anna Coquille, discovered her daughter's cold body lying, still fully dressed, upon her bed. She could make no sense of what she was looking at. How could Hanss have died from a procedure so simple a barber could have done it? How could she have made her way home if something had gone wrong?

How could she have made it up the stairs to her bedroom but lost her strength before undressing for bed? None of it made any sense. So she immediately went to the doctor for answers. Marcel claimed complete ignorance. He had completed the procedure without a single complaint from Hanss and sent her on her merry way. It made no sense at all given what Anna had seen. She turned to the other doctors of Paris to help her make sense of things. An autopsy was performed, and high levels of morphine were discovered in the dead woman's blood. Perhaps not enough of an overdose to kill her, but quite possibly a contributing factor in her death. The coroner postponed the poor woman's burial until a full investigation could be completed, but it seemed that there simply was not enough evidence that the morphine had been administered by Doctor Petiot to assign any blame to him. He claimed to have given only a local anaesthetic, and that was the official account that was filed. Hanss was lowered into the ground after a closed casket funeral as a result of all the probing and passed time. The corpse was already well on its way to decomposition. Once again, consequences slipped by Marcel without leaving a mark. From each brush with danger, he seemed to take away the same lesson: he was invincible.

In 1935, he faced his first investigation for narcotics violations. One of his patients had been turned against him after all of these years and was speaking openly about the many addictive substances Marcel had plied him with to ensure a steady supply of francs continued to make their way into his pockets. This unfortunate man had managed to shake himself free of his many addictions and now hoped to stop others from travelling down the same painful path where he had been led astray. He spoke out on the evils of not only the medicines that Petiot had prescribed, but the ones that doctors all across France were handing out freely to anyone who requested them. He was a crusader, trying to bring addiction to an end. His campaign ended abruptly.

He was found in his rented room overdosed on morphine, much like every other one of Marcel's victims to date. It was possible that he had succumbed to temptation and injected it himself. One of the other doctors who had provided him with drugs through the years might have taken matters into their own hands before this little nobody could damage the reputation of any upstanding medical professional. All of these things might have been, but there could be no denying that Marcel knew where the man lived, had ready access to the medicine that was used to kill him, and had more than sufficient motive. Yet none of these things were sufficient to raise a case against him. The complaint was dropped since the complainant was deceased, and Marcel pressed on to greater good fortune.

In early 1936, Marcel was appointed "médecin d'état-civil" for the 9th arrondissement, giving him the authority and obligation to sign death certificates for anyone who died within that part of the city. It would have seemed the sort of position that it would be impossible to exploit for personal gain, beyond the new standing that it offered him, but Marcel swiftly began using his home visits to the recently deceased as an opportunity to pilfer anything of value that he could find. Often, relatives filed complaints with the police about their officers making off with treasured family belongings, but it did not occur to anyone that the perpetrator might actually be Petiot. He was a wealthy doctor in good standing, so there was no conceivable reason that he might steal such trinkets as were going missing. To do such a thing and risk his comfortable position was unthinkable.

Yet by August of that year, the unthinkable had occurred. Marcel was caught shoplifting a book that he could have easily purchased, and when a police officer was called in to apprehend him, the timid looking doctor suddenly lashed out, knocking the policeman to the ground before fleeing.

For two days following that attack, he vanished entirely, until finally, with his wife by his side, he turned himself in to the local constabulary. His case was unusual enough that he was brought swiftly to court, and there he explained himself using a bizarre concocted tale that blended truth and fiction so seamlessly they were practically indecipherable from one another. He could not be held responsible for his actions as a result of his insanity. The well-documented insanity that anyone with access to court records would have no trouble discovering. While he claimed that his post-war symptoms had mostly abated, he had been plagued by a recent mania regarding a suction machine that was placed against the anus in an attempt to cure constipation. Excessive use of this machine had unbalanced his mind, and as a result, he had been confused about where he was when he had slipped the book that he fully believed to be his own property into his pocket. Furthermore, when a police officer was incredibly rude to him, he had not recognised the man's uniform and lashed out as he would have at anyone else trying to manhandle him. To his twisted logic, he was the victim of these circumstances, and not the perpetrator.

The court was forced to acknowledge that his history of mental health was certainly a factor in his actions. Indeed, he seemed quite clearly deranged when recounting his fanciful tale of vacuum machines and confused book ownership. So long as he sought treatment for his condition, there was no need for criminal charges to be pressed.

His wife, Georgette, gratefully booked him into a private sanatorium, where it was hoped by everyone involved that he would make a swift recovery.

Nobody could have accounted for just how swift his recovery would be. After only a single night in his pleasant little room, Marcel approached a doctor to discuss his release. As a medical man himself, he had the full use of a vocabulary of terms that the general public would never encounter, and it was not long before those doctors he encountered caught themselves talking to him as though he were one of their peers rather than the patient in question.

He explained in no uncertain terms that his period of mental instability had passed already, and that he felt quite ready to return to polite society. He also acknowledged that the doctors needed to do their due diligence and observe him for a few days to ensure that whatever had upset his emotional control was resolved.

Over a long weekend, every one of the doctors that met Petiot became convinced that the insanity that had been his defence plea was a mere invention that he had used to avoid the charges against him. Yet they were not judge, jury, or executioner, and they could not keep a man in captivity simply because he had deceived the court.

In the end, Dr Rogues de Fursac was the primary clinician tasked with determining Marcel's sanity, and while all of his compatriots believed that Marcel was simply a clever liar, he had taken the time to read through all of his patient's history before engaging with him. There were mental illnesses that terminology had not yet been developed for, and de Fursac believed that Petiot suffered from a "chronic unbalance" within his mind. Yet the infancy of his field of study left him with no choice but to recommend that the man be released. There was nothing that their science could prove was wrong with him despite all that the files told of the constant recurrence of his inexplicable criminal behaviour. Without a single theory tying all of these actions together, there was nothing that Petiot could be diagnosed with.

Still, the courts were not satisfied. They assigned their own panel of three doctors to examine Marcel before he could be released. This slowed down the process considerably as each doctor had to observe him in their facility at their own pace. It was almost autumn by the time that they delivered their findings to the court. Petiot was as healthy as he had ever been. They did not believe that he had acted in good faith for a single moment since the beginning of the process, deliberately manipulating the court system and every doctor that he encountered so that he could get the result that he wanted, but he was not certifiably insane in a way that would require commitment to a more permanent facility. So, his victory and vindication finally arrived, much too late for him to take any joy in them.

It took weeks for him to get his business affairs back in order and months before the rumours of where he had been to die down, and even then his reputation as a doctor was permanently tarnished. The celebrity clientele that he had once enjoyed now seemed reluctant to make their appointments, and his other usual regular sources of income began to dry up, too. He refused to perform abortions, to sell drugs to anyone that asked, or to do anything that might see him incarcerated once more. To the outside observer, it probably seemed that he was chastened by his experience and intent upon improving himself. In truth, he was simply furious that he had been caught out and never meant to allow anyone to come so close to ruining him again.

One final insult added to the injury was that the news of his diagnosis had been passed along to the disability pensions office, so the regular income that he received from them was finally cut off. If he was healthy enough to re-join society and function, then he had no more need for governmental support.

Just as he had felt betrayed by military command when he was sent back to the front lines after his injury, now Marcel felt that the civilian government had abandoned him in no less cruel a way. He raged against them internally and began to commit the one crime that was guaranteed not to make him look like he was insane, the same crime that every doctor that he knew in Paris committed with regularity. He began to commit tax fraud.

Where before he had failed to declare income from his illegal enterprises, now he constantly insisted to the tax collectors that he was in a state of penury. He was a doctor, operating out of an expensive building in an expensive neighbourhood of the 9th, but he reported only a fraction of the money that he made on his filings. It did not take long before he was back in court once more. He fought every step of the way, arguing his case using bizarre, fanciful, and convoluted logic that had no chance of being successful but did an excellent job of tying up the court's attention for weeks at a time.

He was fined and sentenced to several weeks in prison for this latest crime, but as his appeals continued to drag on and on and on, the court eventually consented to remove the custodial sentence if he would just go away. Feeling victorious, and still paying considerably less in fines than he would have been due to pay in tax, Marcel was flying high.

Yet there were forces at work in the world that were far larger and more dangerous than Marcel Petiot and his petty struggles with local government. In September of 1939, Germany invaded Poland in the first demonstration of their Blitzkrieg tactics to the world at large, and the Second World War began.

Acts of War

The Phoney War stretched out for eight months after the invasion of Poland as both sides of the global conflict held back, circling and trying to take the measure of the other's capabilities. Naval blockades filled the seas of Europe as economic warfare was conducted and supplies of materiel for the German war effort were disrupted. Only a single military action on land was conducted, with French troops invading Germany's Saar district.

The Saar offensive intended to seize as much territory as possible while the German troops were still entrenched in Poland. The Saar region was held by the German First Army, but intelligence had passed to the French that they were operating on a skeleton crew. If the region could be taken, then any fortifications that the Germans had in place to prevent a large allied incursion into their homeland could be circumvented, and the whole country could be gutted and the war ended as swiftly as it began.

Unfortunately, the French command were still fighting the last Great War when it came to tactics. They felt certain that stationary artillery would remain a deciding factor in any conflict, and the reliance on that slow-moving and slow-deploying equipment, much of which had to be hauled out of storage before the invasion could even begin, meant that their army moved at a crawl.

In the previous war, this attack would have been a roaring success, but faced with contemporary tactics and a rapidly developing situation, they had no hope. The German Blitzkrieg swept through Poland at a pace that nobody could have foreseen, crushing all of their defences with overwhelming force. The Polish desperately needed for the German forces to be divided before they were overrun, but the slow deployment of the French assault and Britain's continual dithering over where to place their troops swallowed up those vital moments when things could have been turned around. With Poland defeated impossibly fast, German reinforcements poured back into the Fatherland, and the French offensive was crushed by overwhelming numbers. They retreated back across the Maginot Line into their own territory.

More conflicts sprang to life across Europe, breaking the concentration of the German war effort enough that the counterblow was slow in coming. But when it finally arrived, it was devastating. The Germans invaded Holland, Belgium and France in one massive coordinated attack that applied equal pressure on every one of the Eastern fronts – a sustained pressure that meant no part of the defences could be reinforced with troops from elsewhere.

Step by step, the French were driven back, bleeding for every inch of ceded territory until finally their lines broke and the German war machine roared to life, plunging through the gap and overrunning supply lines and countryside. In June of 1940, fearing massive loss of civilian life, the military commander of Paris declared it an "open city" and made no attempt to stop the impending German occupation. With Paris lost, so too fell the government of France.

A collaborationist government under Marshal Philippe Pétain was organized in Vichy and broadcast orders for a general cease-fire, which over 40,000 French soldiers obeyed, surrendering to German forces on June 22.

Yet this was not the end of France's fighting by far. An organised resistance was formed of spies, soldiers, and civilians to drive the invaders out, and guerrilla warfare began.

In this new world, Marcel awoke in occupied Paris, opportunities abounding and a new enemy to loathe right on his doorstep. With his contacts in both high society and the criminal underworld, it took him no time at all to make contact with the Resistance, and then his life's work truly began.

German collaborators were known as "Flies" in the parlance of the resistance, so the newly minted "Dr Eugene" elected to call his hastily constructed spy network "Fly-Tox," after a popular insecticide. With his medical practice, he had an ideal nexus for all the people from various walks of life that he employed. Somewhere they could visit regularly to deliver their reports without arousing any suspicion.

French soldiers returning from the front where the Germans had redeployed them to serve as slave labour would be shunted from the public hospitals into Marcel's spare bedroom, where he would tend to their wounds, get them fighting fit, extract all possible information about troop movements to convey to his underground allies, and then sign a disability certificate claiming that they could not return to duty and needed to be released. It was not long before whispers spread and every injured Frenchman wanted him to care for them. He was selective about who he arranged to have slip into his hands. Only men that might provide valuable intelligence could expect the free pass that a highly respected doctor like Petiot could provide them.

But of course, none of this was Dr Eugene's passion. The network was named after a famous poison for a reason. The many drug addicts in the city that had relied upon his benevolence throughout the years found that their favourite doctor was now open for business as normal, and the extortionate rates that he charged could be easily bartered down with a little information on the identities of any people seen visiting the secret Gestapo offices that had been spotted around the city. Petiot loathed the Nazis, certainly, but he reserved a special hatred for collaborators.

His role as spymaster precluded him from any involvement in direct action against the collaborators he discovered himself, but there were patrician fighters throughout the city who could easily assassinate a collaborator or two in between their missions. Fly-Tox performed its role admirably, chipping away at the Gestapo's attempts to establish their own intelligence network and never quite drawing enough attention to bring the full weight of an investigation down upon themselves. Yet still, it was not enough for Marcel.

He began concocting elaborate stories about his heroics in the fight against the occupation, stories so farcical that many discounted the possibility of them being lies simply because the purpose of a lie is to be believable, and the stories he told were anything but.

According to his tall tales, Marcel worked to develop secret weapons that could kill Nazis without leaving any forensic evidence. After a long day of developing scientifically impossible weapons, he would spend his evenings in meetings with the Allied Commanders, who he name-dropped in conversations as readily as others might mention their own family members. If the world was as Marcel described, then there was not a single safe street in all of Paris, given the sheer volume of bombs and booby traps that he had personally placed to disrupt the German war efforts. Though, of course, he might have found enough hours in the day for all of this thanks to the support of the gang of anti-fascist Spaniards that he claimed were operating in the city.

Needless to say, all of this injured his credibility with his compatriots to the degree that some people began to doubt if the man were even a part of the Resistance at all – something that came in particularly useful when the Gestapo began hunting for the Fly-Tox network and the mysterious Doctor Eugene who was its mastermind. Nobody took anything that Marcel said seriously, whether it was true or false, so when interviews were conducted or agents of the Nazi regime asked questions about him, he never seemed a credible suspect. It allowed him to slip right through their fingers.

From his work falsifying disability papers for returning soldiers, he soon turned his attention to falsifying them for anyone who could match his price. The Jewish community soon became great fans of his, and it did not take long before the constant steady flow of brand new customers began to attract attention to his practice from the quarters where he really would rather have had none. If he meant to keep all of his operations invisible, then a new base of operations would be required.

He was not so clumsy as to open up shop in Le Marais itself, where the Jewish population of the city had always resided, but instead chose a private mansion on the complete opposite side of the city, on the east side of the Seine, on the Rue Le Suer, in the 16th arrondissement. It was a far grander building than he had any use for, and the upmarket neighbourhood around it made it all the more likely that odd comings and goings would draw attention, but he had been pulling in so much money from his various schemes over the past few months since the occupation began that he felt like treating himself.

It was with that huge empty space at his disposal that Marcel finally struck upon the plan to line his pockets that would live on in infamy throughout the ages. Until now, his murders had been sparse and only by necessity, to protect himself from the repercussions of his other criminal activities, but now for the very first time, he considered beginning to kill wholesale.

As a doctor, he couldn't do such a thing, not in a career conducted so openly – it would destroy his reputation and his livelihood if his patients disappeared or died. But as the spymaster of the Fly-Tox network, anything and everything that he did was in secret, and anyone who came upon evidence of his evil deeds would assume that they were done in service to the greater cause and question him no more.

The scheme was very simple. There were a great many people in Paris who no longer wished to be there – people who were desperate to escape Nazi occupation and would pay a substantial amount to have a safe way out. In addition to the money that he could demand as payment, each and every one of these fleeing people would be carrying the full sum of all their wealth on their body, as it would not be possible for them to start a new life elsewhere without it. All that he needed to do to extract the full value from them was to kill them. Anyone who cared about them would already be expecting them to disappear and would endeavour to cover their tracks, making Marcel's job even easier. It was the perfect crime, assuming that he felt no compassion or loyalty to the people of Paris.

By way of explanation for his ingenious escape route, Marcel turned back to some of his old lies, spinning them anew. His anti-fascist friends in Spain would provide a route through to Portugal, where those who were escaping Paris would then be able to take a ship to the Americas – more specifically Argentina.

Turning loose his network of petty criminals to spread the word of this grand opportunity, Marcel soon began to see a whole new clientele flocking to his second home. The wealthy but afraid, the truly desperate, the criminals seeking to escape the reach of French and German law, all of them came to Doctor Eugene for the ultimate cure to all of their woes.

The procedure was quite simple. At a set time, those who wished to vanish would arrive individually at the house on the Rue Le Suer. They would bring with them 2500 francs to pay for their passage, along with any luggage or valuables that they did not want to leave for the Nazis to rifle through once their absence was noted. Then Doctor Eugene would explain their journey to them, how they would travel across land to Portugal in the safe hands of an anti-fascist Spanish troupe, and then depart on a ship to distant Argentina where the locals would welcome them with open arms, provided all of their papers were in order. The Doctor had, of course, already prepared all of the necessary papers to ensure that his subjects would receive a hearty welcome, so long as they had undergone all of their inoculations.

"Inoculations?" they would ask, already so overburdened with the torrent of information that Marcel had inflicted on them that they could scarcely even parse the words any more. Then he would inform them of how health-conscious the government of Argentina was, how worried they were about another pandemic of a disease like the Spanish Flu, which had so devastated their country. Nobody was allowed into Argentina if they did not have a clean bill of health from a doctor that they could trust, which was why Marcel was involved in the whole process. To ensure that he was as good as his word, the doctor would then offer up his services in providing the vaccinations that would allow their passage to go on unhindered. Not one of them declined. Compared to the degradations and dread of occupied Paris, what was a little scratch with a needle?

He injected cyanide. Later, when his supplies of that poison ran low, he would use home-grown digitalis extract to stop their hearts, or simply flood their system with so much morphine that they passed away peacefully. He was never short on drugs, even when supply lines were being strangled by the war still raging beyond the city's walls.

Among the first to avail themselves of this new service were a trio of pimps named Joseph Réocreux, Francois Albertini, and

Adriene Estébétéguy. The three had graduated from their usual bottom-feeding behaviour to a new class of crime only recently, when they acquired Gestapo uniforms for themselves and wore them while conducting armed robberies, preying on their own people in much the same way that Marcel did. He learned all of this from Joseph when he arrived at the house on Rue Le Suer in the company of his mistress, Claudia Chamoux. Breaking the clearly set rules and enraging Petiot, Albertini arrived at the same time to make his own arrangements, dragging along Annette Basset, one of the many prostitutes in his employ – a girl for whom he had some affection but also meant to put to work for him again when they arrived in Argentina.

Marcel took their money, injected them with his cure-all, and waited until their bodies had stopped twitching on his floor before rifling through their belongings, stripping them down, and then casting their corpses down the stairs into the basement to be dealt with later.

The next day, Adriene arrived with his girlfriend and employee, Giséle Rossny. The two of them received identical treatment after expressing their surprise at how thoroughly Marcel had made their compatriots disappear.

Those first few bodies were weighted with iron chains and cast into the Seine to sink to the bottom and be devoured by the catfish, but it soon became clear to Marcel that murder on a wholesale scale was going to require more efficient means of disposal. If he threw as many bodies into the Seine as he intended to create, then the mighty river would soon be dammed, not to mention all of the issues of public health and hygiene it would create, issues that he would have to resolve in his daytime life as Marcel Petiot.

So it was that Maurice received a call from his brother for the first time since the war had broken out. He was quite overwhelmed with his important work in the capital, and he needed someone to help him fetch vital medical supplies. Would Maurice answer the call when Mother France cried out for aid?

Entirely used to his brother's theatrics by this point, Maurice simply asked what he was collecting, where he was taking it and whether Marcel meant to pay for his vital supplies in advance or if this was an elaborate attempt to make his poor brother foot the bill. As it turned out, the quicklime that he had been sent to collect was all paid for by mail, well in advance of his arrival, and though he had no clue what use the foul-smelling stuff had to the practice of medicine, he had never pretended to be a doctor and accepted Marcel at his word that it would be used for medicinal purposes.

He had no clue why he was delivering it on the opposite end of town from Marcel's famous practice, but when his brother was the one to answer the door and to actually get his hands dirty helping Maurice to carry the sacks in, it quickly assuaged all of his worries. Marcel even insisted on paying Maurice for his time and travel, thanking him so profusely that it actually took Maurice aback, and he soon made his excuses to head back home.

In the basement, Marcel dug a pit which he filled with quicklime. Into that, he would cast bodies, in parts, to be dissolved. For anything that the lime could not eat through, there was a grand old incinerator in the mansion's basement, which he soon started loading up with fragments of bone and leftover material. Anything that he could not use or sell, he destroyed to eliminate any trace of evidence that might be used against him. Even some of the things that he could have sold, he destroyed in the same manner if he worried that they were too distinctive and might draw the pawnshop owner's attentions.

Despite all of this, word soon began to spread about his network. The lowlifes and criminals that he employed were more interested in getting as many people as possible funnelled to Doctor Eugene so that they would receive their bonuses than in maintaining the integrity of the Fly-Tox network.

By April of 1943, Gestapo agent Robert Jodkum was in charge of collecting information about Resistance groups operating in Paris. He had not personally experienced any negative effects from the Fly-Tox operations against collaborators in the employ of the Gestapo and had little concern for any French that lost their lives due to their own clumsiness, but he did have a great deal of interest in the idea that there might be a passage allowing undesirables to escape him.

His process for ferreting out this little warren of enemies to the Reich was simple. His own agent, a blackmailed French Jew named Yvan Dreyfus, would make contact with the mysterious Doctor Eugene for information about the passage to South America, then he would report back to Jodkum with any details that would help to identify this mysterious doctor, the route that he was taking people out of the city, and any other groups that were offering him assistance. Dreyfus seemed to be the perfect agent to Jodkum. He had a long-standing and impeccable history in the local community, had shown no inclination towards collaboration before he was blackmailed, and had never been seen in contact with any of the Gestapo's agents.

When he vanished, Jodkum was gobsmacked. The obvious answer to Dreyfus's vanishing was that he had been outed as a spy and dealt with as a traitor should be, but Jodkum could not understand how they had caught him out. He knew practically nothing, he was well versed in the things that he had to say to earn their trust, and he had a pocketful of the Reich's cash. There was no reason for him to have been assassinated. Yet he had been. This Doctor Eugene moved up considerably in the Gestapo's estimations after that, and the once farcical Fly-Tox Resistance group went from being a footnote in the reports on more notable operatives and became a file in itself.

The French Police gradually became aware that there was a murderer at large. Body parts washed up in the Seine, some dismembered by sharp knives, others chewed loose by the catfish in the canals. Regardless, it was not long before the waters were trawled, and more and more pieces were discovered. The majority of these bodies would never be identified. Among the pieces were nine decapitated heads of unknown origin, four thighs, and sundry other parts, too. The litany of the dead seemed to show no connection between any of the victims. It was as though they were chosen and butchered entirely at random.

First, there was Nelly-Denise Hotin. A pregnant newlywed who had gone missing when she set out to seek an illegal abortion. Doctor Petiot had fumbled the procedure, and rather than run the risk of the girl fleeing to a hospital when she would not stop bleeding and exposing him for the operations he had resumed, he chose to end her life and dispose of her himself.

Dr Paul-Leon Braunberger was an elderly Jewish man who had planned to flee occupied Paris with his wife. She too had gone missing, but no trace of her was found in the river. He had last been seen on a subway station, heading away from home to some unknown destination in town. For a time, the family had suspected that he had somehow run afoul of the occupying German forces, but it did not make any sense. The Germans were entirely forthright in their hatred and enjoyed making a public spectacle of the murders of civilians that they committed all too frequently. It was all a part of their plan to keep the French people cowed. Yet Paul-Leon had vanished without a trace until he was hauled up in a net.

A family of three German Jewish refugees, the Knellers, were discovered with all of their dismembered parts mixed together. They had attended a consultation with Dr Eugene about travelling even farther so that the Reich could never catch up to them, and then they had blinked out of existence. Three more refugees, the Wolff family, were the next to be discovered. They had come to Dr Eugene with six friends from back home in tow, all of them desperate to escape from the depravities that the Nazis meant to inflict upon them. One by one, Dr Eugene had seen them. One by one they had vanished. More recently, another pimp, Joseph Piereschi, and his mistress, Joséphine-Aimée Grippay, had come to Dr Eugene to escape from the warrants that were out for his arrest, and like the rest of them, he was dismembered and cast into the Seine.

Of the body parts recovered, none comprised the full sum of parts required to make a whole person. Quicklime and fire had handled the majority of the victims that had come into Marcel's care, with the later drops in the river mostly comprising nothing but the leftovers that he could not fit into either the furnace or the pit.

The French were desperately seeking this murderer, but the Gestapo had no real interest in the case. Perhaps if their blackmailed agent, Yvan Dreyfus, had been so clumsily disposed of, then they would have felt more strongly about the corpses in the city's waterway, but they had bigger fish to fry. The hunt for "Dr Eugene" was on.

Of Spiders and Flies

Marcel's illicit activities with his spy network had rapidly become the most profitable of his businesses, and with his usual gusto, he began widely advertising them to any and all who might be interested. This naturally put the Fly-Tox network in a position of vulnerability to Gestapo infiltration.

A French informer named Charles Beretta managed to make contact with lower ranking Fly-Tox members and soon assumed duties spying on the Gestapo offices to take note of other informers like himself. He fed the names of those that he interacted with within the organization back to the Gestapo, and soon the majority of low-level operatives involved in the spying side of things were identified. Of course, the Nazis had considerably more interest in the other parts of the apparatus. They wanted the names of those who committed the acts of violence and sabotage against them. They wanted to learn about the route by which Fly-Tox was smuggling so many enemies of the regime out of France. The name of "Dr Eugene" was already known to them, but despite his best efforts, Beretta could not get close to the man himself so that his true identity could be learned. Dr Eugene remained a mysterious, almost mythical figure, and given what had happened the last time that the Gestapo sent an agent directly up against him, they were not inclined to push their luck with Beretta when he was still providing helpful intelligence.

By May of 1943, the Gestapo were losing their patience. Subtle measures were proving to be unsuccessful, and yet more suspected Resistance supporters had been vanishing without a trace. To make matters worse, suspicions were mounting that Fly-Tox had some sort of sympathisers or connections back in Germany. Requests for information were denied or lost. It seemed impossible to the local Gestapo that some small-time Resistance cell could have somehow gained a foothold in their own apparatus, but it provided the spark of fear that was the impetus for their next moves.

The three highest ranking Fly-Tox members that Beretta had managed to identify were taken into custody: Raoul Fourrier, Edmond Pintard, and René-Gustave Nézonde. They vanished off the face of the earth, as far as their allies could tell, and it would not be until many months later that the truth of their confinement came out. All three men were subjected to torture at the hands of the Gestapo. Their captors were painfully aware that the absence of three key players in the network would invariably lead to massive disruption, potentially rendering any information that they did manage to extract useless in a short period of time. They went at the three resistance fighters with a ferocity unmatched in their usual interrogations. None of the men could offer up any information about other Resistance operations; none of them could explain how Fly-Tox was getting people out of occupied

France. Despite their being the most senior members of the network, the only person who had contact with those other operations was the leader of their cell: Dr Eugene.

So it was that the full fury of the torturers was turned to the end of discovering Eugene's identity. There was a loyalty among the men who served Dr Eugene that was almost cultish. The more that they were tormented by the Nazis in their desperate attempts to identify Dr Eugene, the more believable all the tall tales that the man had told through the years seemed. If he was not the mastermind behind assassinations, sabotage, and communications with the allied forces, then why would the Nazis be so desperate to apprehend him? The harder that they pushed, the more Petiot's loyal followers resisted. These were not the soft men that the Gestapo were used to encountering in France. All three were veteran soldiers of the Great War and career criminals when they were not in that service. They were not men unaccustomed to suffering.

Yet even tough men have their limitations. One by one, they were broken by the Gestapo torturers, and one by one they offered up the name of the man who they served. Marcel Petiot.

He was abducted from his home and practice by the Gestapo in broad daylight, hauled off through the streets in clear view of the whole of Paris. Nothing could have better certified his credentials as a member of the Resistance to those who had doubted him before. His home and practice were thoroughly searched for any sign of his Fly-Tox operations, but the radios and communications equipment that the Nazis expected to find were nowhere to be seen. There were no cyphers to break allied codes. There were no communications details for other cells. Nothing that might have helped the Gestapo was anywhere to be found. They knew nothing about Petiot's other property in Paris because the Fly-Tox men knew nothing about it.

From the outset, the Gestapo were convinced that they had been duped. There was no way that this odd, nervous little doctor could have been the leader of the Resistance. Of course, they were scientific in their methodology. They applied pressure to determine if the man would break, and what they would get if he did break. Marcel denied any knowledge about the Fly-Tox network, knowing that admitting knowledge of it would lead immediately to his death, but beyond that, he was free and easy, sharing any information that he had with his interrogators. He would have said or done anything that they wanted to get out of the prison at Fresnes. He would have sold his own mother to the Nazis if it meant he could avoid even the gentlest of punishments. This was the kind of response that the Gestapo had expected from the rest of Fly-Tox, the kind of craven behaviour that they associated with the French in general. But still, there remained the hope that this was all just another layer of deception, that Petiot was in fact Dr Eugene, and they had cut the head from the viper in their midst.

Once more, the other three Fly-Tox agents were put to torture with demands for any information about Dr Eugene that might help prove or disprove Petiot's connection to the nom de guerre. All three men were insistent that Petiot was their man. They were certain that he was the one.

Stretching their web of informants wider, the Gestapo collated all information that they had about Resistance groups in Paris and presented details from them to Petiot, seeking proof that he was connected to them. Marcel offered up everything that he knew in an instant, but what he knew amounted to nothing. His stories may have painted him as a well-connected genius agent provocateur, but the truth was that he had done little of what he claimed. His ignorance protected him throughout all the verbal traps that the Nazis sprung during his interrogation.

For months, Marcel and the other three men were held and tortured daily, yet by the end of it, the Gestapo were no further forward in their investigation than they had been at the beginning. If Marcel Petiot was lying to them, he was one of the most accomplished liars in human history. Eventually, the Gestapo simply concluded that he was a patsy for the real Dr Eugene, a false identity provided to his supporters so that they could throw pursuit off track. It was obvious to the Gestapo that the weedy man that they had in custody could not have achieved any of the ridiculously heroic exploits that they had heard tell of Eugene accomplishing, so they cut all four men loose in January of 1944.

The admiration of Dr Eugene after managing to withstand eight months of torture at the hands of the Gestapo was almost comedically over the top. Everyone in the Fly-Tox network now hung on his every word. Every story that they had considered farcical before now seemed plausible in the face of the man who had given not a single Resistance member away in eight months. As for the other three men, Petiot welcomed them back with open arms. They were only men – they could not be expected to resist torture forever. The others in the network may have lost respect for them after they turned over Marcel to their mutual enemies, but they were still tolerated at the request of Dr Eugene.

He could not have had more devoted followers after that, and though the three of them could no longer spy due to their cover being blown, Fourrier, Pintard, and Nézonde were now the doctor's most devoted helpers in all other matters, no matter how depraved or appalling they might have appeared. With a renewed vigour, and greatly increased trust being placed in him by the real Resistance fighters of Paris, it was not long before Fly-Tox had their refugee smuggling route back in action, and the money flowed as steadily as the Seine through Marcel's front door. In the weeks that followed, it seemed as though an almost impossible number of people vanished from Paris, travelling via Dr Eugene to parts unknown. The Gestapo's active-target lists seemed to dwindle more and more every day, but they still felt certain that Marcel Petiot could not possibly be behind it. He could not have fooled them so thoroughly. They were certain of it. Even though his release perfectly coincided with the resumption of Fly-Tox's activities, they felt sure that it was all part of the same grand ruse that had placed Petiot in their sights to begin with. And so the months rolled on, and so more and more people died at the good doctor's hand. As many died in those months as he had slaughtered in all of the time prior to his capture by the Gestapo. His new reputation as a hero of the Resistance had rapidly spread, winning over all who had doubted him before. Even the outlandish tales that he had told about himself spread among the Resistance and through holes in their security to the Gestapo. A hunt was undertaken for the Spanish anti-fascists who were now suspected to be in operation in the city. The natural deaths of Nazi supporters and soldiers in Paris were re-opened for examination to determine if they had been the victims of the infamous Dr

Eugene's invisible assassination methods. Every lie that he had told on a whim became another thread in the vast tapestry of his legend, which the Nazis were trying and failing to construct and follow back to the source.

As the old tall tales were recycled and repurposed to boost the faltering morale of the resistance, long-forgotten lies saw the light of day once more. The idea that so much information was flooding out from the Resistance forces of the Fly-Tox network that the workings of the German war machine were being undermined became a commonplace belief. Indeed, the tide of war was turning against the Axis powers by this time, and given how little the occupying forces were told about what was happening further afield, they soon found themselves certain in the belief that the mysterious Resistance heroes were truly turning the tide of war.

There were some among the Fly-Tox network who had known Petiot before the war. Vicious criminals who had made use of this doctor's credibility to support their own schemes. Among them, Petiot had now developed an entirely different kind of reputation. They did not believe for a moment that he was involved in the noble efforts of the real Resistance, nor that he had some secret route out of France. When their blatant disregard for his lies became apparent, Petiot had no other option than to take them into his confidence and make use of them. They were the men he had carting away stolen goods by the truckload for resale. They were the men who helped him to dispose of corpses, butchering them for burning or to scatter their remains in the quicklime pit. These were the men who watched as he snipped off fingers so that rings could be more easily retrieved, who watched him play the strings of his informants and "spy network" like a concert harpist. His reputation among them was not as a hero, but as the "king of crime." They had never seen a man commit such brazen acts without any sign of morality. They had never encountered a man of such intellect who devoted it not to the betterment of mankind, but solely to himself.

As with many wealthy men, it seemed that there was no limit to Petiot's greed, and no real use for all of the money that he had acquired. The cash piled up with nothing to spend it on, and while his family were treated to every comfort imaginable, there was nothing that he could provide to them or himself with his newly acquired riches that he had not been able to offer with his successful medical career. He collected more money simply because he wanted more, not because it made any difference in his life. When he lost money due to the costs of doing illegal business, or simply because of poor fortune, he was quick to shrug it off and move on. Everything he was working for was ultimately meaningless. He wanted the feeling of success that came with hoarding wealth without ever having any purpose for it. Even if by some happenstance he did suddenly crave the intensely luxurious lifestyle that all that money could bring him, there was nowhere in occupied Paris that it could be spent. Supply lines were strangled by the war. That was half the reason many of the upper class visitors to the Fly-Tox escape route came – because they were tired of living like common people when they could be luxuriating in their own wealth elsewhere.

Funnily enough, if he had been freely spending his money, then it was likely that it would have drawn attention locally and his illicit enterprise would have been discovered, but once more, Marcel's obsessions protected him from the consequences of his actions.

It should come as no surprise that in the end, Marcel Petiot was not exposed by the cunning efforts of the Gestapo counter-intelligence network, or by the diligent investigative work of the French Police. His sense of grandeur was his undoing. His insistence on purchasing only the finest property in Paris put his charnel house in immediate proximity to the wealthiest citizens and, therefore, those who were the most concerned with appearances as well as with the state of their local neighbourhood. These were neighbours who had no need to work and could not indulge in their usual proclivities for travel during the occupation, so they soon discovered a new passion for gossip and observation of the comings and goings of their odd new neighbour, Dr Petiot.

He had guests arriving at all times of day and night. He had trucks pulling up, loading and unloading things as though this were some dockyard. He was never there to be told off, and when he was there, it was at odd hours when it would be impolite to confront him. Not to mention the guests. So many of them, from all walks of life, with no unifying factor that any of the neighbours could tell. At first, they thought that perhaps he was running some private practice from his home away from home, but these did not seem to be sickly people. Nor would sickly people show up carting all of their luggage with them. It made not a jot of sense, and before long, every one of his neighbours was quite desperate to know just what was going on behind the doors of that house. To make matters even more pressing, there were a whole variety of unpleasant smells constantly erupting from the house. Decay and burning were the prominent ones, but also odd chemical reeks that made neighbours wonder if Petiot might be operating a distillery or something similarly lowbrow out of his living space.

Multiple reports were made to the police about the foul aromas escaping from the house, and each time that officers visited, they were bombarded with tales of Petiot's odd behaviours. It was soon filed away among those working-class men of the force as harassment. The neighbourhood resented the nouveau riche like Petiot, and this was their attempt to drum him out. Attendance at the nuisance calls became less and less frequent until finally, it seemed that Marcel could do literally anything in that house without the police taking notice, simply because the neighbours had cried wolf one time too many.

On the Sixth of March, 1944, the other residents were finally availed with an opportunity to get past this blockade. Vile, oily black smoke had perpetually poured from the chimney of 21 Rue La Sueur, day and night, with no considerations for how it might impact dinner parties or the like, but now it was observed to also be escaping from some of the upper story windows. Attempts to rouse the inhabitants proved to be entirely fruitless, and a note was discovered, written in the hand of Marcel Petiot, explaining that he would be away for a month, and that in the case of any emergencies, he could be contacted at his office across town.

It was the ideal opportunity to get the doors of the place open and shine a little light on the matter. The police were called and immediately fired off a telegram to the doctor, warning him that there appeared to be a fire out of control at his property. He shot back a response immediately that probably caused more alarm than the fire itself. "Do not enter the property, I will be there shortly."

The police were understandably suspicious but had no desire to enrage a private citizen in good standing, so they held back. Moreover, they suspected that Petiot had been on the receiving end of a great deal of subtle abuse from his neighbours, so they wished to give him the benefit of the doubt in dealing with this situation.

More and more smoke poured out from the house as the police stood there waiting. Almost half an hour after the reply telegram had been received, the police were forced to take action by growing concern that the fire was spreading. They did what they could to move nosy neighbours back out of sight, then called for aid.

The fire brigade arrived rapidly and forced entry to the house via the second story, where windows were already open to allow smoke to escape. They were intent on putting out whatever fire was raging and ending the danger as swiftly as possible. The police and the neighbourhood waited patiently outside as the moments ticked by and the foul black smoke still came boiling out through the windows. Inside they could hear shouting. The smoke still poured forth. More shouting, screams. By now the police were stepping forward, ready to force entry on the ground floor and offer whatever aid was needed to their brothers in uniform, but even as they came closer, the fire-fighters came flying out of the front door of the house, rushed to the garden, and vomited wildly. Needless to say, it was enough to catch the attention of everyone in attendance. The policemen quickly went to their aid, but there was no consoling them. Between sobs, retching, and coughing, the firemen managed to mumble out some beginnings of an explanation, then just like that, the police were off to investigate for themselves.

Inside the house, they were confronted with a scene from a nightmare. Thick black smoke was billowing up, not from an uncontrolled fire, but from a series of wood-burning stoves throughout the property that were stocked to bursting not with wood, but with limbs. That smoke made it impossible to see anything in the house until the policemen were tripping over it. They crashed into the sparse furniture as they tried to make their way around. They were getting separated and lost in the omnipresent dimness of the smoke. Heading up the stairs, one officer tripped over a sack that had been left lying there casually, and a whole human head came tumbling out of it to bounce down to the entrance hall. Through the kitchen to the rear of the house, a flight of stairs led down to more scenes of depravity. In the basement, where the furnace was blasting at full pelt consuming larger body parts, they discovered a pit filled with quicklime and decay. More bodies than any of the policemen had ever encountered were littered through the home. There were suitcases full of the deceased's belongings, too. In the garage space, a fresh pit had been dug and heaped with bodies, the quicklime all made up and ready to be poured over it.

In the other rooms, they came upon something like a factory line of corpses. First, they were stripped of their belongings, then of their clothes. Further along, gold fillings were yanked free and rings cut loose of fingers, then finally at the end of the room closest to the kitchen, there was a heap of butchered bodies waiting to be transferred to the fires and the pits. This was not mere murder – it was methodical processing of corpses. It was the sort of thing being committed in concentration camps throughout Nazi Germany and beyond, though public knowledge of them and the Holocaust would not be spread until many years later. Without that frame of reference, only Medieval depictions of Hell seemed to be sufficient for their descriptions.

Rapid interviews with the neighbours established that quicklime was most likely being delivered by night, when the luggage was retrieved and taken elsewhere. The sheer number of the dead was overwhelming, and also impossible to quantify. There were so few whole bodies within the entire building.

In the midst of all this, Marcel Petiot strode in and took command of the situation. At once, he sought out the highest-ranking police officer on the scene and had him gather his men. They were all so horrified by what they had seen, so shaken loose from any sense of reality, that they all went along with it. Petiot demanded to know who else had been informed of their discovery and showed visible relief that it was only the men still around the house. He then took pains to ensure that every officer on the scene was a fellow Frenchman before he seemed to relax.

Taking the poor sergeant aside, he explained that he was a part of the Resistance, and that the bodies they had discovered belonged to Nazi agents and collaborators that he had killed for the cause. It was an outlandish, ridiculous claim given the volume of the dead, but given no other sane reason why anyone might have killed so many people, they almost believed it. They detained Marcel while they tried to work out how his story could be verified. None of them had any desire to interfere with the brutal and grotesque work that the Resistance were forced to undertake to set their nation free of the occupation, but neither could they understand how what Marcel had been doing here could in any way help the cause.

They were paralysed by indecision, until once again, Marcel was saved by his enemies.

The Gestapo had learned of the state of the house through their spy network, given that the neighbours who had heard a little of it were gossiping frantically. They immediately issued a warrant for Marcel's arrest, along with all the information that they had about him following his confinement in their prison, right down to a mugshot of him in their secret prison. Along with the warrant came a proclamation that Marcel Petiot was a dangerous psychopath who must be stopped at all costs. Exactly the kind of thing that the Gestapo would say to try and win support from the local police if they were trying to capture an enemy spy.

So convinced, the police let Marcel leave, wishing him well and pretending that he had never arrived at the house. When the Gestapo came swarming in to take over the scene of the crime, the French police gladly stepped back, telling nothing to anyone. It was a decision that they would later regret.

For days, the case was in limbo, belonging to neither the German investigators nor the French police. News of the slaughterhouse had spread rapidly and appeared in all of the local papers, but nobody knew what to make of it. Was this the work of the Resistance? Was this the work of the Gestapo? Could some random man who had passed the citizens of Paris by every day have committed these atrocious acts without any higher calling?

Once it became clear to the Gestapo that none of their agents or collaborators could be found among the dead, they abandoned the case into the care of the locals.

A veteran legend of the French police, Commissaire Georges-Victor Massu, took charge of the investigation once it was established that the dead were not Gestapo agents but private citizens – almost exclusively Jewish private citizens. To begin with, this left the French police with the distinct impression that they were dealing with a collaborator and agent of the Nazi powers, killing for the enemy. The declaration that had been issued, along with the warrant for his arrest, convinced them that this was not the case, but this also introduced a whole new layer of confusion. If Marcel was not working for the enemy, then what possible purpose could these killings have?

In an attempt to make sense of it, Massu dug into Marcel's past, seeking out his connection to the Resistance, or the Gestapo, and hunting for whatever reason the Germans might have had to turn on their agent.

Marcel's pension was a matter of public record, as was his venerated service during the Great War and the patriotic vigour with which he had attempted to drive out the Germans at every turn. All of these things pointed to his being a Resistance agent, yet the few contacts that Massu had within the Resistance denied all knowledge of this Doctor Eugene.

The Fly-Tox network soon came to his attention, and he reached out to the known members of that group, seeking any sort of logic behind what had been discovered. Their devotion to their leader remained, but Massu was also a legend in his own right, and gradually information about the activities of the group were shared. Most pressingly for Massu, the idea that the network had a supposedly invisible way in which French citizens were being vanished from sight. With horror, they consulted what few records Fly-Tox had kept on the citizens that they had saved. A full accounting of them all was held only by Marcel Petiot himself, in his diary, but bits and pieces had filtered out to the rest of his network, and the names and faces were rapidly pieced together with the pieces of people still remaining in the charnel house. Everyone that they believed to have been smuggled out of the country was dead.

Massu concluded that he was dealing with a truly twisted mind, but he needed more information before he could use that knowledge to his advantage in hunting Marcel Petiot down.

Digging further back into Marcel's history, murders began to come to light that had not even been detected at the time: the addicts who had come forward to identify Petiot as their supplier and then mysteriously gone missing, the patients and the witnesses who had simply disappeared when they went against him. A pattern began to emerge of a man who would kill for petty gain, to avoid inconvenience, or simply because he felt it was expedient.

One of the bodies recovered from the charnel house was identified as Jean-Marc Van Bever, a drug addict who had admitted to the courts that he had procured his illegal prescriptions from Dr Petiot shortly before vanishing in the midst of his trial.

A second body was identified as that of Marthe Khait. Her son had been one of the addicts that Marcel procured drugs for, but during a police crackdown on illegal pharmaceuticals, he was arrested. Many of the prescriptions that Petiot had written for the man were in his mother's name, so he was swift to contact her and offer a way to weaken the prosecution's case, against both her son and himself. All that she had to do was lie under oath, claiming that the prescriptions were both legitimate and for her health issues. At first, Marthe readily agreed to anything that might shield her baby from the law, but after consulting with her own doctor, who insisted that there was no way the court would believe her lies given the medications involved, she reversed her position and set off to tell the truth in the hopes that honesty might win her some sympathy from the jury. She vanished before she could make that testimony.

Later, her husband had received a pair of letters informing him that Marthe meant to leave the country. Consulting with the Fly-Tox network only confirmed to him that she had abandoned her family to escape Nazi occupation. Her son was not so gullible. He reported his mother as missing to the police, but no trace of her was ever found. Not until her body was pulled from the quicklime pit.

Beyond the tales that the bodies told, there were so many more suspicious deaths that had happened in Marcel's orbit. There were his childhood outbursts, his teenage confinements, and his pre-war behaviour to take into account. Even back then, there were a few deaths dotted here and there that could be attributable to a young budding psychopath if you were to look at them right. Then in the chaos of the Great War, with death all around him, there was so much opportunity for this kind of evil to slip through the cracks. The records of Petiot's stays in mental institutes became available to Massu, and from them, he began to construct what we would now call a psychological profile, but what at the time was merely an attempt to discern motive in the madness.

The crimes that Marcel Petiot had been accused of in the past were not violent, and it would have been ridiculous to assume that every man who committed a little fraud would also be a mass murderer, yet from Petiot's actions back during his political career, Massu was able to discern the seed that would one day flourish into this tree of wickedness: the desperate obsessive desire for more. To have more. To hoard more. To be more. It all informed Petiot's actions.

So, with a motive in mind, and the beginnings of an idea as to the methodology used in the mass killings, Massu began to make arrests.

Georgette Petiot was brought in for questioning. Her extravagant lifestyle put under the microscope. She knew that Marcel was making a great deal of money, but she assumed that it was through business dealings and his position as a medical examiner that so much wealth was flowing into the home. She had never questioned the gifts of dresses and furs, jewellery, and perfumes. She lived a relatively charmed life as Marcel's bride and the mother to his children, and she knew that he worked long hours to provide for them, sometimes not even returning home for days at a time.

It took a great deal of questioning before she could even countenance the crimes that her husband was being accused of, and even when she did grasp what was being suggested, she could not believe it of her sweet Marcel. It would not be until many months later when more of the victims were identified, that Georgette's personal belongings – the gifts from her doting husband – were entered as evidence against him. Stolen from the corpses of his victims. Even then she tried to convince herself that there was merely some mistake. That her husband could never have committed such vile acts. The original intention had been to arrest and hold Georgette as a willing accessory to the crimes of her husband, but as time went on and more and more of the story of their life together came out, it became more apparent that Marcel had neatly partitioned his life in two, with his wife and family on one side of the divide and his slaughterhouse and business dealings on the other. Georgette was released – though she still needed a police escort for quite some time, thanks to an unfortunate snap of her in the local papers.

Still, the police were not content to allow the members of the Petiot family of which they knew the location roam free. Georgette may not have been a guilty party, but someone had been driving the vans from out of town that were delivering the materials that Marcel used to dispose of his victim's bodies, and when he was questioned about his comings and goings, Maurice readily admitted to helping his brother. Yes, he had delivered quicklime to his brother's new address. No, he didn't know what it was used for, something medical, he assumed? Or perhaps to do with Marcel's job working with dead bodies. He'd never had much interest in his brother's business dealings, but if Marcel was willing to pay well for his time, then Maurice was happy to help out. The police did not believe this flippancy. Maurice was jailed as a co-conspirator and his name dragged through the dirt, all because he'd driven a truck for his brother a couple of times when the man didn't have time to fetch a delivery for himself. It hardly seemed fair.

As for Marcel's most devoted accomplices within the Fly-Tox network, the three men who had been jailed along with him by the Gestapo were rounded up and put to question. Once they had established that Massu was a patriot, through and through, they readily admitted to all that they had done in the service of the Resistance. They were zealots, committed to the dogma of Marcel Petiot's Fly-Tox network. Where there was no good and evil, only the great cause. The freedom of France.

Those who were more criminal in their inclinations avoided being taken by Massu, preferring to blend back into the French underworld, while the ones who presented themselves readily to make statements in Marcel's defence were the most devoted and deceived of his followers, who gladly admitted to operating the charnel house on the Rue Le Suer. They were all jailed for their complicity in the crimes. The law cared nothing for the motivations of a murderer, only for the act that had been committed. It meant nothing that these men had been deceived into thinking black was white and up was down. All that mattered was that they had acted on those beliefs in a way that produced such monstrous results. The fact that they had been so free with their confessions made it all the easier to compose a proper case against Marcel. These followers had no reason to think that there was any need to hide any part of their operations from fellow Frenchmen, so they spilt every secret that they had ever been told.

From there, Massu led a search of Marcel's apartment on Rue Caumartin. It had been abandoned, with nothing taken, not even the substantial sums of ready money that the man had lied about. Marcel kept in his home a massive surplus of medical supplies, far beyond what any practicing doctor could ever need. Some of it, the police were certain, was intended for sale on the black market, but there were other things that nobody in their right mind would purchase and certainly wouldn't seek to purchase in such vast quantities.

Massive amounts of chloroform were discovered, a veritable wine cellar's worth of the drug that could render victims unconscious if they were forced to inhale it. It had proscribed uses for a medical doctor, but no doctor, no matter whether it was war time or not, could ever feasibly use as much as Marcel had hoarded.

With that discovery, a deeply unsettling revelation came over Massu. These massive amounts of chloroform were almost certainly being used to incapacitate Petiot's victims before they were dragged off to be destroyed, but given the brutality of every other part of the operation, Massu now had to contend with the idea that those who were butchered may still have been alive as they were stripped and sliced apart. They might very well have felt it rather than the desecration being post-mortem.

The fabled diary containing a full list of all Marcel's appointments and victims was nowhere to be found in either house, not that the police had hoped to have such luck. A call had been sent out through the city for friends and family of the missing to present themselves at the morgue in the hopes that either the remaining parts or some keepsakes still held in Rue Le Sueur might provide some enlightenment regarding the victims' names.

The final discovery that the police made at Petiot's home was a garden. Not containing the usual flowers found in such places, but instead a wide variety of poisonous plants. The most prevalent was digitalis, commonly known as foxglove, there being many planters scattered around the balconies of Petiot's upscale residence containing them. The soil around their roots had been disturbed. The fluid that was produced in the root ball bulbs had been extracted with the syringes still left lying around. A poison potent enough to stop a man's heart with only a small dose, and Petiot had been manufacturing it on such a scale that he could have killed half the populace of Paris if given sufficient time. It went beyond simple criminality and into the realm of the bizarre. Why any man should want to kill so many people was beyond Massu's understanding.

So faced with a level of evil that he could not even understand, he turned to the most evil men he could conceive of for assistance.

Robert Jodkum was in charge of the investigation on the Nazi side, and he readily shared all available information with Massu, further cementing the investigator's belief that Petiot could not be an enemy agent. Jodkum remained unclear on exactly what had led him to initially pursue Petiot, but he did admit to the reason for the monster's previous bout of incarceration. He had been held on suspicion of smuggling Jews out of France.

When this little snippet became public knowledge, rather than just a myth being spread around by Resistance groups, Massu was able to launch his appeal to anyone who might have previously sought out "Dr Eugene's" services. The police found a man who had abandoned his plan to flee when Petiot informed him that the steep price of passage to South America was 2500 francs. His tight purse strings saved his life. Others came forward who had brushed against Petiot's escape network, some who hadn't been able to meet his price, others who had simply felt that the offer was too good to be true. It was all that Massu could do to keep the story under wraps so that any genuine underground routes out of occupied territory wouldn't be tarred with the same brush. The Gestapo felt the same way, although for different reasons – they could not admit that any route out of France existed lest people begin searching for it.

So, with all of Petiot's past now laid out on paper, Massu turned to the present and the future. With the connections that he had made, it would have been a simple matter for Petiot to escape the city. The question that plagued the authorities was not if he had fled, but where he would have fled to.

The general assumption was that Petiot would be heading for a neutral country. The Resistance had passed information about this murder out to the Allies, and the Gestapo were fuming over the way that he had thumbed his nose at their power. Discovery in either one's territory was liable to end in blood.

There was a certain assumption among the regular police that Petiot would already be well on his way to South America through the escape route that he had so often bragged of, but Massu recognised the very existence of such a route as a lie from the outset. Petiot's plans were just as easily carried out with a false promise of safety as with a genuine escape route.

Marcel Petiot's picture was passed out around the ports of France. The border checkpoints were forewarned to expect him and to search any vehicle heading out of Paris as it was likely that his cultish followers would smuggle him out despite any risk to themselves. All of this was snapped into place as quickly as was possible, and given that the Gestapo were trying to help rather than hinder the investigation, the barrier that was raised around France should have been more than fast enough to catch him. All of France waited with bated breath for Marcel to make his escape attempt. All of the world was looking for him. Yet he still did not appear. In theory, the authorities had constructed a dragnet that no man would be able to escape, but for some reason it was not having the desired effect. Either Marcel had already escaped France in the day before such defences could be raised, or he had managed to slip through their fingers. With each passing day, Massu began to second guess and doubt himself more. This was all reaching a fever pitch when once again a change on the world stage had its impact.

Operation Overlord had been planned by the Allied Powers for many months, and in June of 1944, it was finally launched. A 1,200-plane strong airborne assault on the beaches of Normandy pounded the Nazi emplacements with bombing while over 5,000 ships brought in ground troops for an amphibious assault. Nearly 160,000 troops crossed the channel from England on that first day, with more and more following until there were two million allied troops on the ground in France by the end of the month.

Whatever plans the French police might have had were blasted apart. Whatever hope they might have had of controlling the movement of people in and out of Paris was obliterated. With so many bodies milling about the countryside, Marcel Petiot could quite literally have just strolled away from the consequences of his actions if he so chose. He had plenty of money, and he had criminal contacts around the world – it would have been a simple matter for him to flee and never face any sort of criminal charges.

Yet despite all of the reasons that he should go, it seems that Marcel Petiot was not yet done with France. Whether it was patriotic fervour, excitement to see sovereignty restored to his people, or simply his ongoing belief that he was above such petty things as consequences, he remained.

The Hunt

Loyalty kept him alive. Even though he was a liar and a killer, and even the Resistance was hunting him, Marcel Petiot always had friends and patients who would ensure his safety. In the early months of his life as a fugitive, he was constantly on the move, smuggled from one safe house to the next under cover of darkness, but gradually those who gave him shelter lost their faith. They wanted to believe in the hero of the Resistance, they wanted to protect him from harm after all that he had done for France, but when the whole world was announcing his evil, from the Nazis to the French police to the Resistance itself, it was difficult to believe his rather shaky stories. Particularly as he looked more savage and bizarre with each new house he came to, growing in a thick beard and wild hair to help disguise his identity.

Eventually he settled into relative safety in the home of Georges Redouté, a man who was singularly disconnected from all of the gossip of Paris yet maintained a healthy respect for Petiot as the doctor who had saved his life. Petiot convinced him that he was wanted by the Gestapo for killing Nazis and informers. Of course, Redouté was ready and willing to help when that was the only version of the story presented to him. Petiot's actions throughout his confinement with Redouté only served to convince the man that his one-time doctor was legitimate. Marcel left the house only at night and returned in the early hours of the morning with weapons that he claimed to have taken from German patrols.

History went marching on outside the walls of Redouté's house. The French police went on strike and found themselves trapped inside their stations by German tanks. The Allies worked in partnership with the real Resistance to drive the Nazis back. In August 1944, it seemed that a tipping point had been reached when Marcel's cover story of hiding from the Gestapo would no longer be sufficient to explain his continuing need to hide from the public sight. In appearance, Marcel Petiot could very well have been a new man on the first day that he stepped out into the streets of Paris by daylight. Combined with some new paperwork that his criminal conspirators had conjured up for him, his thick beard, near starvation, and newly greying hair completely shrouded his identity.

Henri Valeri needed a job to survive, of course, and while the fraudulent papers were of excellent quality, they would not be sufficient to allow the practice of medicine. Instead, Marcel fell back onto his other skill set as an accomplished soldier. He joined the French Forces of the Interior, a newly assembled army meant to push back against the Nazi forces still at bay within France, and given his experience and abilities, he was immediately offered a commission as Captain. His skills from his days in the Resistance were the most highly in demand, however, and his captaincy involved considerably less parading around on horseback and considerably more counter-espionage and interrogation of prisoners. Every prisoner in the Reuilly district was under his jurisdiction, and whatever means he saw fit to extract information from them was considered a small price to pay if it meant that the occupying forces could be run out of France once and for all.

There were a great many deaths under torture, and a great deal of respect for Captain Valeri for his willingness to do whatever was necessary to thwart the invaders. The fact that so many of those who died gave up no useful information, and that several were, in fact, men who had known Marcel Petiot and needed to be eliminated so that their knowledge could not be passed on, was purely coincidental.

By September, the capital was entirely purged of Nazi infiltrators and was finally considered to be liberated. Captain Valeri's attentions were now required elsewhere. He would set out from Paris to comb the surrounding area for any sign of espionage.

Funds had been tight since he had to abandon his old life, and now Petiot saw the opportunity to balance the books back in his favour. The world beyond Paris was rife with chaos and opportunity for plunder. Opportunities that Petiot was more than happy to avail himself of. Many homes had been abandoned during the war, and he and his troops had the perfect cover to go raking through them in search of Nazi agents left behind – along with the perfect excuse for any items gone missing. The Germans must have taken them.

Soon Henri Valeri became one of the wealthiest men to be on a mere Captain's wages. His unit operated in the area around Paris for the most part, so it was simple for them to shuffle stolen goods back into the City of Lights and the waiting shadowy underbelly populated by Petiot's old contacts, who could transform anything into ready cash.

For months, his troops picked the countryside surrounding Paris clean. The things that could not be sold for ready money were passed along to the black market, where such things could be readily dispersed to those who had no desire to live within the limitations of rationing. He received a cut from everything that was sold and soon positioned himself and his soldiers as unofficial bouncers for the market. Anyone attempting to double-cross one of his sellers would soon find themselves picked up for questioning regarding their collaboration with the Germans during the occupation, and while these investigations came to nothing due to there being no evidence, just the accusation was sufficient to completely destroy a reputation.

The only time that he came close to his illicit activities being uncovered was when he deployed two of his most loyal soldiers to the home of the Mayor of Tessancourt. In addition to over twelve million francs in cash and rare stamps, they came upon the owner of the property, the Mayor himself, who was none too happy to be on the receiving end of such blatant burglary. With no instruction from their commanding officer on what to do when confronted, the two men attempted to flee the scene, pursued by the elderly gentleman until it became apparent that he was not going to let them go unchallenged. At which point, they emptied their machine guns into him.

They had waited too long to take action. There were witnesses to their crime out in the street, and those same witnesses, three young men from Tessancourt, ran to the FFI command to warn them that they had thieves and murderers in their midst. They were greeted by Captain Valeri, who immediately tossed all three of them into one of the jails he controlled and threw away the metaphorical key. One of the FFI lieutenants who had encountered the witnesses began his own investigation, until he was directly ordered by Henri Valeri to abandon his work and let things lie. It was widely known that Valeri was the spymaster for the FFI, dealing in the dreadful secretive work of counterintelligence and espionage. If he claimed that a good man with no mark against his name deserved to be murdered, then that spoke to the victim's character, not the spymaster's.

Once more, Petiot had asserted his control over the situation, and his confidence alone had managed to assuage all doubts. The two men who stood accused of robbery and murder vanished without a trace, and while it would normally fall to their commanding officer to order an investigation and have military police root them out for deserting, Captain Valeri elected not to. Once more, it was an odd enough decision to warrant comment and questions, but his unique role shielded him from serious scrutiny. The truth of the matter was that his superiors were honourable men who wanted to know as little as possible about the dirty business of spycraft and left him entirely to his own devices when they could.

So Petiot was rendered invisible in this new life he had invented for himself, and he would have been able to pass completely unnoticed into the annals of history – if only he had not been so proud.

The Parisian newspaper Résistance published a story about the odious deeds of one Marcel Petiot just a few days after the murder of the Mayor of Tessancourt. In it, they described him as a "soldier of the Reich" who, they claimed, had dressed himself up in a Nazi uniform before hunting French Patriots around Avignon back in March of 1943. Something patently untrue but guaranteed to rile up the sentiments of the people of France against him like little else could.

The story of Petiot's murders had not escaped the public eye before this point, but it was the first time that his story appeared in a publication that he had any respect for. Shortly after the discovery of the bodies in his charnel house, the local newspapers had run stories dubbing him "The Butcher of Paris," the "Scalper of Etoile," the "Demonic Ogre," and his most famous nom de guerre, "Doctor Satan." It was headline news in those first few days, and it was juicy enough a tale that it soon spread worldwide, appearing on front covers around Europe, where it was assumed that he might have taken shelter. Later soubriquets included "The Modern Bluebeard," "The Underground Assassin," and when connections were made to his work in the Resistance, "The Werewolf of Paris." It was a media circus, but one that was constantly being interrupted by larger events worldwide so that it could not be brought to the usual fever pitch. Now that it seemed the war in France was over, it would not be long before journalists ran out of news and turned back to the tale of Doctor Satan to sell their papers.

A few days after the publication, a letter arrived on the doorstep of René Floriot. René was an attorney who had served as Petiot's legal defender in one of the previous cases brought against him relating to the illegal supply of drugs. He was as close to a "family lawyer" as was likely to be found. In the letter, his fugitive erstwhile client declared his innocence and stated that the story published in Resistancé was a fabrication that was being perpetuated by the Germans. A collection of "filthy Kraut lies."

There was, understandably, no return address upon this letter, and no real demand for legal action to be taken against Resistancé for slandering the good doctor's name. However, Petiot made a fatal mistake in writing to his lawyer about it. Resistancé only had a circulation of Paris. It was not sent farther afield, it was not reprinted for other markets. The only way that Petiot could have read the story about himself, and responded to it in such a short time, was if he was still in the city of Paris himself.

The newly reformed police did not have the manpower to undertake the hunt for this dangerous lunatic themselves, even though there was massive public support for his capture now that the war was coming to an end and more accurate reporting of his crimes was finally coming to light. So they turned to their brothers in the FFI for assistance, and the FFI turned to the man best equipped to hunt down lone agents of evil hiding in plain sight: Captain Henri Valeri.

Valeri set out at once to make as large a noise as possible, producing a frankly ridiculous amount of leads for other departments to pursue while sending his soldiers on wild goose chases all through the city, chasing down witnesses or informants that he knew had no direct connection to Petiot because he had never heard of them.

It was such a contrast to the usual subtlety with which he approached his missions that others in the FFI began to suspect that he was deliberately sabotaging the investigation. Those who had already bought into the mystique of their spymaster Valeri thought that it meant that there was more involved in the Petiot case than had been made public knowledge, that perhaps Valeri knew about some secret arrangement that had been made to protect Petiot as an agent of a foreign allied power. The rest of the FFI thought that Valeri was a petulant minor officer throwing a tantrum over being given a job outside of his usual remit. After only a short month of terrible investigation, it was that second group that saw to his removal from the job.

Henri railed against that decision, but he could not provide sufficient reason that he should remain on the task force when there was so much other work needing to be done. The man who had been able to walk out of police custody with a few terse words, who had been able to talk his victims into rolling up their sleeves to receive a lethal dose of poison, the career politician who had been able to shout his way out of fraud and corruption charges, had finally found a situation that he could not talk his way out of.

Eyes were beginning to turn to Valeri now that he had marked himself as less than perfect. Attention was being given to his past service, and in time, he felt certain that his papers might finally be examined by someone who did not have an inherent bias in favour of believing his lies. He had pushed himself into the spotlight during the hunt for Petiot, and now he frantically backpedalled to escape it.

Having seen the forces now arrayed against him from inside the belly of the beast, Petiot began making plans and enquiries about leaving both Paris and France. Plans that had to be made in utmost secrecy since there was no possibility that Henri Valeri would ever contemplate abandoning his post.

Finally, when he felt that scrutiny within the FFI was becoming too much, he took the plunge, shaving off his beard to make Valeri disappear and then making a break for it.

Vanishing back into the Parisian underworld, he made good use of the few criminal contacts who knew him as both of his personas to acquire all the material that he needed to make a break for it and set himself up in comfort somewhere else.

On October 31, Petiot was sighted at a Paris metro station. The police were summoned, and he was arrested just before he could climb aboard a train and vanish once more. He made no attempt to resist arrest, nor to flee, as he felt both of those things might harm the legal defence that he had already begun preparing. In his possession at the time of his arrest was a pistol, over thirty thousand francs, and fifty different sets of identity documents with his picture attached – a whole cornucopia of alternate identities that to this day still have not been fully investigated. It was clear from the outset that he could have fled France at any time and disappeared so thoroughly that he would never have been found again. Yet he had chosen to remain – he had chosen to believe in his own ludicrous stories.

He genuinely believed that his role in the resistance to Nazi occupation would be enough to absolve him of absolutely everything. That political allies would come out of the woodwork to protect him from the consequences of his actions, or to disclose that he had done his work for them. He believed it with such certainty that he made full confessions to his crimes while incarcerated, chatting away with Massu as though the two of them were old war buddies, and the entire situation was just a misunderstanding. For his part, Massu was able to stomach acting as though he were merely composing a report rather than preparing to nail Petiot on more murder charges than had ever been filed against a single man.

Clear Conscience

Nobody came to Petiot's rescue. No mysterious benefactor swept down to carry him away. He was sent to La Sánte prison to await trial, claiming absolute innocence. After a brief period of hoping that figurative angels might descend from the heavens to protect him, he succumbed to doubt and enlisted the services of René Floriot to represent him in court once more.

Floriot had one hell of a task laid out before him. More or less the entire world had heard about Petiot's crimes by this point. With the war over, any hope that the chaos of the conflict might provide a smokescreen evaporated. To make matters worse, a lawyer in France couldn't enter any sort of plea, or argument, that did not reflect the express wishes of their client. An insanity plea probably would have found solid footing given Marcel's medical history in that regard as well as the sheer obscenity of the crimes that he was charged with. However, this was not the approach that Marcel wished to pursue. He insisted that patriotism be his only defence. He insisted that everyone that he killed was an enemy of France, that they were all collaborators, that they were all a part of the occupying force. It was no longer clear whether he believed this was his best defence, or if he had truly come to believe his own lies and delusions. The result was the same: an abject insistence that he was a hero and that the courts were fools for standing judgement on his actions.

Needless to say, the case was theatrical in its scale. The courtroom was packed to bursting with family members of his victims and the press, queued out into the rest of the building and spilling out into the streets outside. On Petiot's side of the courtroom sat Floriot. On the other side were a crack team of state prosecutors, backed up by twelve civil lawyers who had been hired by relatives of his victims. Even if the case were not already so drastically weighted against him, the overwhelming legal expertise of his opposition could quite easily have wiped the floor with him. Public opinion, the true turning point on most trials by jury, was already so stacked against Petiot that it was almost pointless proceeding, and his lawyer presented motions to that effect. It would be impossible for Marcel to receive a fair trial given the situation, so it should be deferred until such time as the public's ire against him had cooled.

The three judges of the court rejected such motions. There would never be a time when the world stopped loathing Marcel Petiot, and delaying until such a time as the public outcry ended would be impossible. Still, Floriot went above and beyond what anyone could have expected of the lawyer of such a guilty maniac. While Petiot stood in the box at the rear of the courtroom grinning wildly out at the families of the people he had slaughtered, Floriot called every witness that he could imagine in the man's defence. Every known Resistance leader from Paris during the occupation was brought up in court to testify as to Marcel's whereabouts and duties, and not one of them could do so. It was almost as though the Resistance that Marcel Petiot had worked with did not exist.

Some recognised the man as a hanger-on, a fraud, or someone who was willing to do work for money – but never for the cause – during the occupation, but these moments of recognition did little to help his case now.

Proceedings were delayed yet again as telegrams and letters were sent abroad to all of the foreign intelligence agencies that Petiot claimed to have been funnelling information to, but once more, it was as though the man had never existed. No foreign power might have wanted to get dragged into what could have become a real political mess, but it seemed that the rather more banal reality was that Marcel Petiot was simply a liar.

In desperation, Floriot attempted to pull up the Gestapo reports on the Fly-Tox network. Their offices in Paris had, somewhat inevitably, been put to the flame, and little remained of the extensive paperwork that had once identified Doctor Eugene as a threat to the stability of the Reich. But there were scraps of information along with other prisoners who had briefly cohabited with Marcel during his incarceration who provided enough corroborating information to prove that he was definitely involved in something.

Records of the secret weapons that he had been constructing for the Allies were nowhere to be found. The assassinations he claimed to have conducted upon prominent Nazis had never happened. The bombing forays that he had undertaken to hinder and sabotage the occupation were mysteriously devoid of any recorded explosions. He had assumed that in all of the chaos of war, nothing was being observed, when in fact everything had been meticulously noted and tracked by the real spies who were intent on seeing the Nazis ejected.

So it was that Floriot and Petiot sat down to construct their timeline of events so that Marcel's side of the story could finally be heard.

According to Marcel, the first time that he encountered any dead bodies at all was immediately following his release by the Gestapo. He only became aware of the corpses stowed away in 21 Rue le Sueur in February of 1944, when he returned there, and he was immediately shocked and appalled to discover them. Dead people, in his own home. He was beside himself with horror until he realised that they must have been left here by agents of the Fly-Tox spy network, meaning that they were invariably going to be collaborators and Nazis. After that, he was able to set aside his delicate sensibilities and turn his attentions to the task of disposing of the evidence before he or his comrades in arms could be connected to the villains' disappearances. He called on his brother for aid, and used the quicklime that Maurice delivered to begin the gruesome task of getting rid of the corpses in a pit dug into the basement of the property. When this was proving insufficient to deal with the volume of traitors and enemies heaped up in his home by the invisible and unnamed assassins, he had begun destroying bodies in the fire, too, leading to his discovery. Given that he did not want any of his agents to be exposed, he bravely took the blame for all of the murders and faded away into the underground to continue fighting back against the Nazis until he had the opportunity to take up arms openly against the enemies of France once more as Henri Valeri.

No element of this story could be corroborated in any way, of course, and every attempt that his defence made to find any way to prove its accuracy led to a dead end. The reconstructed timeline fit to known events, but that was the extent of its provable accuracy, and it certainly didn't account for all the corpses in the Seine. To make matters worse, there was the money. Over 200 million francs worth of cash, gold, and jewels were missing, not to mention the small fortune that was retrieved from his private property. In the end, the case proceeded with the assumption that he had killed his victims to plunder their belongings. Twenty-seven victims were listed on the original docket as the identities of so many of the bodies discovered still could not be established. Many would never be identified with complete certainty.

The trial began on March 18, 1946, at the Palais de Justice in Paris, with a seven-man jury to make the final judgement and a panel of three justices to keep the presentation of information in order through what was certain to be a dense and complex case.

Even knowing all that they did about the case coming into it, it was unlikely that the judges had any idea of the circus that they were in for. Not only was the place packed to bursting, but the defendant seemed to be treating the entire proceeding like it was a night at the theatre. Rene Floriot spent the first day of the trial frantically trying to silence his client as he shouted out gibes, mocked the prosecutors and quipped along to the evidence being presented, but by the time that the second day of court was in session, even the judges themselves were getting drawn into bantering with the Doctor.

When witnesses were presented, Petiot himself often ended up grilling them from his box at the back of the courtroom, shouting back and forth to be heard over the hubbub. It did little to convince the court of his innocence, but it did wonders for the entertainment value of the event. It may have been their circus, but it was rapidly becoming apparent that Petiot himself was going to be the star act and poor Floriot the lion tamer trying to keep him under control.

Piece by piece, the prosecution laid out their case against him, and day by day, he decried them all as traitors to France for turning on him so.

The secret weapons that he had been developing during his time with the Resistance he outright refused to discuss on the grounds of national security. The information could only be used against France if he brought it into the public eye, so why would the court want him to? Were they perhaps collaborators with the Nazis, still intent on bringing about another Fascist invasion? He was censured by the court for making such inflammatory statements, but it certainly set the stage for the rest of the proceedings, where everyone was against him because they were involved in some vast conspiracy.

After the second day of the trial was complete, one of the judges and two of the jurors were overheard by a reporter discussing Petiot's comportment throughout the trial in private, calling him "a demon" and "an appalling murderer." The moment that this information was printed in the Parisian newspapers, Floriot leapt upon it, calling it cause to declare a mistrial. After some discussion among the judges, the two jurors were replaced while the judge, who had been happily calling the defendant exactly the same things, remained in his place on the bench. The trial then proceeded unimpeded.

On the fifth day of the trial, the jurors and judges visited 21 Rue La Sueur. A veritable army of police had to be deployed to ensure Petiot's safety from the gathered crowds of bloodthirsty Parisians baying for justice. Upon hearing his jeering neighbours demanding that he be killed on the spot for his horrific crimes, Marcel simply smiled. "Peculiar homecoming, don't you think?"

One by one, the civil lawyers representing specific victims were bombarded with his abuse as they attempted to present their case against him.

He accused the lawyer of the Khait family of being a "double agent" and a "defender of Jews," which did little to disabuse the public of the idea that he was potentially a Gestapo agent, at least until the evidence of his incarceration and torture at the hands of the Germans came to light. That was a turning point for public opinion when the papers reported and corroborated their evidence. Until then, everyone had assumed that his talk of working against the Nazis had only been talk, but now they were confronted with the very real possibility that the man they had all been baying for the blood of was actually one of the heroes of the Resistance. The fact that none of the other resistance cells knew Marcel as anything other than a joke, or a hanger-on, meant nothing to the papers, who suddenly had a whole new layer of story to explore. Was this man a hero? Was he a monster? Was there some possibility that he was both in one? His stories of wartime heroics seemed more plausible now that his fellow prisoners had accurately identified him, even telling the court that he was suspected of being a leader of a secret network smuggling people out of France. The official account in the Gestapo records had gone up in flames, so now only witnesses could give credence to his tales. And inexplicably, they seemed to.

So it was that the public was teetering on the edge of believing some part of Marcel's story might be true by the time that court was back in session the next day. When discussing victim Joseph Réocreux, he loudly observed that it was easy for any medical man to identify the victim as a collaborator because of the shape of his skull. "He had a head like a pimp, you know." He leered at the officer in the stand providing evidence. "Like a police inspector."

The uproar that followed this little gibe rolled out through the gathered officers and turned into roaring laughter when it hit the public galleries. Over dinner conversations around Paris, the story was told and retold, growing in hilarity with each recounting. There was nothing that the French loved more than wit. It was the quality that helped them to rise above the more brutal peoples of Europe, after all. How could anyone funny possibly be evil?

The next day, the questioning turned to all of the missing people whose belongings were recovered but whose bodies had not been. The civil lawyer called Petiot to the stand and asked him bluntly: Where was Joachim Guschinov if Petiot had not murdered him? Petiot merely smirked and stated that he was alive and well. If that were so, asked the lawyer, why couldn't the prosecutors find him? If he were truly alive and well? Petiot let out a laugh as he answered, "Because South America is a very large place."

Many of the victims that he was accused of murdering were not dead, according to Petiot. The Fly-Tox network had smuggled them safely out of France and they were living new lives under assumed names on the other side of the world. None of them could be found specifically because they had been trained to move frequently and change their names and appearances with each move to avoid any pursuit by the Nazis. One by one, he addressed the civil lawyers, telling them where their post-mortem clients had been shipped off to, how it had been achieved through Portuguese ports, and why they could not now be discovered. In Petiot's opinion, many of the people who had fled abroad and were not making themselves known, were fleeing the debts of their old lives and enjoying their free and comfortable futures in the new world. A future that Petiot jokingly suggested he now wished he had pursued when he had the opportunity rather than devoting himself to saving France, given the repayment he was receiving.

So continued his explanations of where his victims had vanished to – until they reached the Wolffs. The Wolff family were Dutch Jews who had been trying to flee the occupation, but Marcel painted an entirely different picture of them. According to him, they were Germans, and they had returned home to Germany to begin their preparations for the next war against France that was sure to swiftly follow the temporary victory that everyone was so proud of themselves for just barely achieving. It struck a note with the gathered crowd, even if it mostly put the jurors' noses out of joint. There was a general feeling at the time that the tide of war had only temporarily abated, and the implication of Marcel's statement was clear. If they were to go around imprisoning or killing all the people who had been willing to fight and die for France, there would be nobody left to stand up to the Germans when next they came rolling through the gates of Paris. This attitude also lent credence to his reasons for being so reluctant to disclose the vital evidence that might exonerate himself. He would not reveal spies in deep cover, not even to save his own life. It painted him even more clearly as a hero of the Resistance and his prosecutors as short-sighted politicians more interested in making things tidy than dealing with the real consequences of the war.

Similarly, he stated that his victim Kurt Kneller and his family had returned to Germany so that they might ready the next offensive against France. He tossed in a titbit about a particularly embarrassing affliction that Kurt suffered from, but would not disclose more to the giddy newspapermen in the galleries because of doctor-patient confidentiality.

This was an ongoing theme in the trial. He would drop hints at secrets that he would refuse to disclose, building up his mystique while muddying the waters of what was true and false. To begin with, it seemed that he was simply churning out his usual self-aggrandizing nonsense, but as the trial wore on, it became increasingly apparent that this was a deliberate tactic, designed to confuse the jury as to where the truth lay. The fact that his lawyer so readily took up his spurious statements and ran with them was further evidence that this was all a deliberate ploy on Marcel's part. A calculated move that they had agreed upon ahead of time. If they could create enough doubt in the mind of the jury, then the evidence would cease to be damning and merely be adjacent to the larger truth that Petiot claimed was being hidden for the good of all.

From there, things began to deteriorate even further. The only evidence of Marcel's involvement in some of the missing persons cases was that their belongings had been found in his second home, a place that he claimed had been an operating hub for underground Resistance groups throughout the war. Some of the victims he was claimed to have killed may have fled under their own power if they were Resistance fighters themselves. It created more and more doubt about his guilt. Doubt that his defence meant to prey upon.

Dr Paul-Leon Braunberger's clothes had been discovered in the charnel house at Rue Le Sueur, but according to Petiot, he had only met the man for ten minutes at a public luncheon as part of his social duties as a doctor. It was possible, they posited, that Braunberger was a fellow Resistance operative in another cell who had been forced to escape through the Fly-Tox network. It was equally possible that he had turned collaborator, and Resistance assassins had done their duty by removing him. Neither option placed Petiot anywhere near to the site of the man's death – if he was even dead at all.

Throughout all of these proceedings, Petiot – and by extension his lawyer – continued to declare himself a hero of the Resistance, and France. He readily admitted in the course of proceedings that he had killed 19 of the 27 victims himself, stating plainly that they were Germans and collaborators. Dragging the reputation of unfortunate murder victims through the mud for his own aggrandizement. He went on to admit to killing a further sixty-three enemies of France, unbidden by the court, as he began to weave his grand delusion out into a story for the papers. Of the bodies in the house, forty-four remained unidentified, and when asked for comment on them, Petiot glibly told the court, "I do not have to justify myself for murders I'm not accused of committing."

In one final flourish before the closing statements, Petiot got into an argument with head judge, Leser, as he was spotted doodling instead of listening intently to the evidence being presented against him. When rebuked he replied, "I am listening, but this doesn't interest me very much."

The newspapers could not get enough of the demoniacal murderer and his antics, with almost every French paper devoting the front page each day of the trial to the latest comedic hijinks that the man had undertaken in court. Bizarrely, this seemed to win more people over to his cause than any number of tales regarding his wartime heroism. He may very well have been one of the worst mass murderers in French history, but he was also a clown in a time when things looked consistently grim, and people came to love him for it and wished that the trial might continue longer so that more of this curious character might be observed. He was the talk of every café in France as well as of dinner parties at home and abroad.

It was a level of celebrity and public attention that was practically unheard of at the time, and one that would shape how crime was reported in France and globally for decades to come.

So it was that when Floriot stood up in court on the final day of the trial and gave an impassioned speech about the heroism of Petiot and the Resistance, the whole crowd crammed into the peanut gallery burst into applause and cheering for the people's hero. He had turned the tide of public opinion. He had done what many would have considered utterly impossible and charmed the whole world into forgetting the grotesque crimes that he had committed.

All of the world except for the six men in the jury, of course. They had been living each day with the memory of the photographs taken from the scenes of Petiot's crimes burning away at their dreams. Many of them now suffered nightmares and nervous afflictions after seeing the horrors that he had inflicted. They did not care if he was charming or intelligent, or if he could give a quippy answer to every point that the prosecution made. The fact of the matter was that the evidence was so heavily weighted against him from the very beginning that nothing short of a miracle could have turned the case.

The jury was sequestered to deliberate, and once more there was a carnival atmosphere around the courthouse. There was now every expectation that this lunatic Marcel Petiot might end up back on the streets to continue thrilling the public for years to come, that there would be a hung jury and a mistrial, that the sheer volume of charges arrayed against Marcel might overwhelm the jurors, resulting in mistakes and confusion that could stretch out into weeks more coverage. The jury took only three hours to work their way through every single charge on the docket – approximately ninety seconds per charge against him.

He was acquitted on nine of the one-hundred thirty-five counts based on insufficient evidence. The rest he was found to be guilty of. Twenty-six premeditated murders made up the bulk of the charges against him. They were certainly the charges that would have the most influence over the sentencing.

Marcel took the news that he was going to be executed for his crimes against humanity with the same wry smile with which he had absorbed all the other goings-on in the courthouse – as though he had considered it a foregone conclusion from the beginning and was merely taking the opportunity to put on one last grandiose show before he took his final bow and stepped off the world stage.

Immediately, Floriot filed an appeal against the court's decision. In the first, he considered the whole matter to be a mistrial due to Judge Leser's statements regarding his client's guilt at the beginning of the trial. Following such a statement being made public, it would have been more appropriate for a judge to recuse themself from the case than to continue to preside over it.

In addition to this, Floriot insisted that two of the witnesses had perjured themselves by presenting evidence that they could not possibly have been witnesses to. He had objected at the time but had been overruled by the very same Judge Leser, who it was very easy to see as a hostile party to a fair trial at this point in the proceedings.

To the grave misfortune of Marcel Petiot, Judge Leser was a well-respected man among the judges who had to consider the appeal, and while some of them firmly believed that he had behaved in a less than professional manner in the original trial, they did not want to damage the stellar reputation of such a man by bringing his judgement into question. Certainly not to help save the life of a grotesque little sideshow creature like Marcel Petiot. As to the perjuring witnesses, they informed Floriot that unless clear evidence could be provided to contradict the statements of the woman and her maid, then there would be no way for such an appeal to hold up in court. As Floriot had no means of acquiring such evidence, he was forced to admit defeat and convey to Marcel that he had failed in his task.

For his part, the Doctor took the news with surprisingly good humour, thanking Floriot for his diligent work and sending him on his way with instructions to perform no more work on his behalf. He had come to the point in his life when not knowing his fate seemed more fearsome than knowing the moment and means of his destruction.

So Petiot was returned to the prison of La Santé to await his punishment. On the very day that his appeal was rejected by the court, he was hauled out to the ancient edifice in the yard outside the prison. It had been in use since the French Revolution, a creaking piece of machinery riddled with woodworm marks and rust. When his head was placed into the gap between the wooden bars, he was still grinning away as he had been in court, halfway between a cackle and a grimace, as they yanked on the rope and nothing happened at all. The old machinery had given out. The blade had rusted into place and could not be dislodged.

It would be May before a portable guillotine could be transported to the prison and assembled. Just days before this delivery was scheduled to be made, a routine search of Petiot's clothing revealed an unpleasant surprise. It was a small ampule, barely noticeable in the cuff of his trouser leg. The first assumption was that it was cyanide, final evidence that some spy organisation had been supporting him all along and meant for him to take his life painlessly rather than suffering through the indignity of execution. In reality, it was a sedative that he meant to take before mounting the scaffolding and facing death so that he would not feel the bite of the blade or the fear of his impending annihilation. How he had laid hands on such a thing was a question that prompted a great deal of discussion among the guards of La Santé. Typically, a prisoner received contraband through a visitor – Marcel had received none, not even his wife. Or through one of the guards, who in this case universally loathed him to the degree that even the criminal element amongst them would not have done anything to ease his passing. Or, finally, through the other prisoners, who loathed their resident celebrity with such passion that it was not safe for Marcel to mix with the other prisoners during exercise time. In the end, it was decided that the prisoner had smuggled it in himself upon his initial arrival, carrying it with him through his long confinement. It explained why he had no fear of the guillotine. He did not intend to experience it, rather fading off into one of the drug-induced dazes that he had so enjoyed in his youth.

They watched him closely from then on, waiting to see his composure break and fear to set in. Yet even without his drug, it seemed that death did not faze him. He could see the yard through the barred window of his cell, and he watched as the delivery was made and the construction began. It took several hours through the night for the guillotine to be built by the guards, and even once it appeared to be finished and he was set for his execution, things were delayed further as a local engineer was called in to make sure that it would operate correctly. They did not dare to use a faulty machine again in case something went awry and Petiot somehow survived a second time in Madame Guillotine's jaws. So once more, he sat and he waited for his death to come, wide awake in the middle of the night as they made ready for his destruction.

When the guards finally came for him in the dark of the morning on May 25, Marcel greeted them fondly, as though they were old friends, and asked, "When are they going to assassinate me?"

He was offered the opportunity to speak with a priest but declined, stating that he "would rather take my baggage with me." Summoned from his cell, he was offered the traditional glass of rum and a cigarette. He declined the drink, perhaps not wanting anyone to believe that he was attempting to anaesthetise himself after his prior brush with a painless death leading to the guards treating him with such contempt. During this cigarette, some of the more sympathetic staff continued to talk to him, eventually convincing him to meet with the prison chaplain, for his wife's sake at least.

To that man he said, "I am not a religious man, and my conscience is clear." Then he was returned to the tender care of the executioner and the ritual.

The collar of his shirt was carefully cut off and his neck was shaved with a razor. While his hands remained unbound, he was asked to sign the prisoner register, acknowledging how he was departing, which he managed to achieve without a tremor in his hands. Despite themselves, many of the guards found themselves strangely impressed with the man's composure. It seemed that he meant to die a hero's death even if he had not lived a hero's life.

Outside, the witnesses were assembled, including a doctor to ensure that the procedure was carried out successfully. Not that there would be much doubt. On this day, the doctor assigned to the prison was Dr Albert Paul, who was already acquainted with Marcel socially through their time working in Paris as doctors. It is from his diary and observations that we know so much of Marcel Petiot's final moments upon the earth.

He strode with a casual gait up to the guillotine that would soon be severing his neck as though he were entering his own office for a routine appointment. There was a sliding table that he was to be strapped to before being inserted into the machine, so he turned to the witnesses and gave them warning. "Gentlemen, I ask you not to look. This will not be pretty."

Lying down upon the table without complaint, he assisted the guards in getting his wrist straps fastened and still managed to maintain not only his composure but a kind smile for each of the men. He even seemed to have a smile for his executioner in the end, because when the blade fell at 5:05am, his severed head tumbled into the basket with the same wild grin that he had displayed throughout his court proceedings. Doctor Satan was dead.

Secrets and Lies

With the death of this story's main character, you may think that it has come to an end. However, there were a great many unanswered questions following Petiot's final meeting with the guillotine. Despite so much of his wartime behaviour being blatantly self-serving and psychopathic, he did run a successful spy ring, and he did seem to have access to information beyond what might be expected of an individual with no support. For someone so self-centred, it seems ridiculous that he would have put in all the effort that he had without some promise of reward. Not to mention the strong impact of the patriotism that had influenced his earlier life.

Various theories have been put forward regarding the many oddities in Petiot's story, and many of them have been corroborated or confirmed by more recent disclosures as WW2 documents pass the statutory time that they must remain classified.

The first and most obvious question was why the Gestapo back in Germany refused to provide material support to their local counterparts when it came to Marcel Petiot. There have been many theories kicked around through the years as criminologists and historians have tracked this story to its logical conclusions, but the vast majority of primary sources from the time period were destroyed in the days leading up to the end of the Third Reich.

An abiding theory for many years was that the Gestapo benefitted from Petiot's actions and therefore left him to continue to operate. He was spreading fear and confusion in an occupied state, interfering with genuine Resistance efforts, and adding to the general feeling of oppression and terror that helped the Nazis to maintain their power. Not to mention his wholesale slaughter of any Jewish refugees and allies to the Resistance who could no longer take the heat. However, this theory was reliant on the Gestapo being aware of the true nature of Petiot's operations at the time when he was performing his great work of slaughter – something that seems extremely unlikely given how much of his mass-murdering didn't come to light until the final days of the war. This theory likely grew out of the mystique of omniscient surveillance that the Gestapo cultivated throughout the war, but it is unsupported by the evidence.

A more logical explanation, based on what we now know of Petiot's willingness to profit from the war regardless of who was harmed, is that he had previous dealings with German intelligence.

During the first world war, we know that Petiot was stealing material from the French war effort and selling it along. The biggest buyer for battle-ready equipment was, of course, the German army, who were attempting to invade. This might run contrary to the prior state of patriotic fervour that Petiot displayed, but when we remember that by this point, he felt like he had been betrayed by the French army, and that his usual response to betrayal was lashing out in the most destructive manner possible, the idea that he was helping the German war effort becomes considerably more plausible.

In retrospect, it also seems likely that his relocation to Paris may have been related to intelligence gathering for foreign powers. If he was already earning a pension from the German intelligence services from the assistance that he had provided to them so far, it stands to reason that he would continue to offer up fresh information in exchange for more wealth. By the time the Second World War began, it was clear that he no longer had any real allegiance to anyone but himself, and given the level of cognitive dissonance he displayed in all of his decision making, it is quite plausible that he might have been operating an intelligence-gathering programme for the very Gestapo that he seemed to be actively opposing as a part of the Resistance. This would also explain the attempts that he made to wheedle himself into other Resistance groups even though they could provide him with no material advantage in his own pursuits.

If he was an intelligence asset for the Gestapo back in Berlin – and he might have been compromised if that information was shared with the local branch – it seems that the events that followed would have played out exactly as we now know that they did. It would also explain how a doctor living in Paris came by the masses of intelligence regarding German movements beyond the scope of his own intelligence network's operations. He would know everything if he was playing both sides.

Forensic accountancy at the time was not up to the task of backtracking through all of the many years of illicit dealings that Petiot had conducted to confirm whether he was receiving money from the Germans. He was certainly receiving money in excess of the war pension that he had been granted by France throughout his life, but because of the way in which he conducted business, trading cash in hand for his services and charging the government's healthcare fund for the same treatments, his income was always erratic. The fact that he was perpetually bringing in money through embezzlement, sale of stolen goods, and various other business concerns muddied the water further. He certainly was consistently bringing in more money than any of his legitimate interests could provide, but through all the chaos, it was impossible to determine a pattern to his income.

Of course, with the destruction of so many of the Gestapo records from the time, it is now impossible to definitively prove one way or the other that he was working with the Gestapo. However, there is no denying that it would account for many of the discrepancies in the story of Marcel Petiot.

Yet none of this seems to account for his behaviour at the point of capture. For all that he might have spouted off constant self-aggrandizing lies in the manner of many narcissistic sociopaths, he had never shown himself to be so foolish as to believe his own lies before. In the time following his arrest, Marcel genuinely seemed to believe that there would be political intervention on his behalf. It was not the setup for his later defence, though it was certainly integrated into that defence once his wise counsel got involved, but rather seemed to be rooted in an honest belief that someone was looking out for him despite everything that had come to light. What could have convinced a man who was self-made and self-reliant to the point of obsession that some external force would come to his rescue?

Even at the time, the reporters and investigators were confused about the whole situation. In the years that followed his execution, further explorations of the subject were conducted, and favours were called in from the varied Allied nations to see if anyone involved in the covert operations in Europe had any information about Marcel Petiot and his involvement in the war effort. All of these attempts proved fruitless, and the consensus opinion remained that he was just delusional.

That was until 2008, when a cache of America's wartime files was discovered in a barn in Virginia and the truth came out.

Some context is required to understand exactly how a French serial killer and doctor came to be providing vital information to the American war effort, and how the connection could have remained concealed until so recently.

In 1942, Brigadier General Kroner, the head of the War Department's Military Intelligence Service, was given the go-ahead to form his own espionage agency independently of the OSS. The intention behind this move was to provide a secondary layer of protection in case OSS operations were compromised, a function that this new department served ably in the post-war period, identifying many Soviet infiltrators who had taken up roles in the OSS prior to its dissolution.

To lead this new operation, Kroner selected one of his rivals, who had been in the running for head of Military Intelligence before the war, John Grombach. From the 1920s on, Grombach had renounced his French citizenship to pursue a career working in the intelligence services for America, starting at their West Point Military academy and the New York National Guard before officially leaving government service to join the American Olympics boxing team and to pursue a brief but successful stint working for Paramount Pictures and a subsidiary of CBS. Using the international connections he made during the Olympics and his business dealings, he had set up several small intelligence networks across Europe, all feeding directly back to him. While he officially returned to service in the Office of Coordination of Information in 1941, his networks of spies had been funnelling information through him to the OSS and US Government for many years prior to this.

When granted free rein as the new leader of the intelligence agency he dubbed "The "Pond," Grombach immediately turned his attention to counterintelligence at home. He worked with the FBI to collect information on secret communists within the intelligence and law enforcement communities and blackmailed them with knowledge of their political affiliations so that he could gain wider access to not only the information of all other agencies but also to the secret information that was being shared by the communists among themselves – communist groups that were occasionally being fed information and material support from Soviet Russia.

While this seemed to be the sum of the work that the organisation was doing at home, Grombach had over two thousand field personnel through both his own private network of contacts and more recent acquisitions of like-minded anti-communists. Among their number was a doctor named Marcel Petiot.

The Pond operated under its own jurisdiction to the degree that it was not even clear if the President was aware of its existence. The Pond was not formed as a government agency but as a private company, and while it drew over $300,000 as an operational budget from the War Department, it did so as a private consultancy rather than as a part of that department. The extreme secrecy that this provided allowed The Pond to operate entirely undetected for so long that even after wartime operations were wound down, The Pond persisted. To supplement their budget, The Pond invested in foreign businesses within the countries where they were operating, allowing them unfettered on-the-ground reports from all parts of the world. While code names were used for almost everything, obscuring the details even now, it seems likely that Petiot's Paris surgery was financed in some part by an investment from The Pond.

Initially, Petiot was passing along gossip that he had gathered from his patients and what little snippets he could gather of military operations, but once the occupation of France began, his efforts kicked into overdrive. His treatment of French soldiers from the front lines gave him unfettered access to troop movements, and his spies keeping watch on the local Gestapo provided other American agents in Paris with a safeguard.

Providing another explanation for the reluctance of Berlin to investigate him, or possibly lending credence to the theory that he was already in contact with a Nazi intelligence operation, Marcel Petiot was contacted by Abwehr operatives in Paris when they needed medical treatment. These German spies came to him initially for emergencies, but he soon became the regular doctor of almost every one of them. The

Abwehr and Gestapo had different spheres of influence, but it is quite possible that the Gestapo back in Berlin had been told to leave him alone as he was working with the Abwehr, or simply given an ultimatum in regards to him. Either way, by the time that Marcel emerged from Gestapo custody, he received an ever-greater influx of Abwehr agents and was paid well for his services, possibly as a sort of apology from his benefactors in Berlin.

This opened up a whole new realm of possibility for his spying work. The Abwehr believed him to be a trusted ally and spoke openly among themselves of their work both in Paris and abroad. From them, he was able to ascertain considerable information about the deployment of German spies in America, which was then passed along to The Pond, and from there to the FBI.

As a result of Petiot's information, dozens of Abwehr agents were discovered living as normal people in the USA, some in sensitive jobs, some in academia, all of them ably reporting back to the Reich regarding the state of things in America. Many of these spies were arrested or killed, but a great many more were willing to swap sides, providing false information to Germany and feeding back what information they could gather in exchange for their lives and freedom.

While Operation Paperclip, whereby Nazis were given a clean slate in exchange for working for the USA, was still just a distant dream, Nazi operatives were still being taken into the care of the American intelligence services. Ultimately, Grombach did not consider the German fascists to be the true enemy of America. He was convinced that the USSR and communism were always going to be the greater threat, and for this reason, he was more than willing to work with the

Germans towards equitable peace accords, even when that was not the stated goal of the United States.

Starting in 1942, Grombach worked with a defected Soviet intelligence officer to identify Soviet agents in the OSS, ultimately leading to that agency's dissolution. He continued his campaign against communism in all forms after the second world war had ended and Petiot was taken into custody.

If Grombach had any personal feelings about the discovery that one of his foreign operatives was a mass-murdering psychopath, then he never committed them to paper. Indeed, it seems quite likely, given the level of secrecy that The Pond functioned under, that he never thought Petiot's connection to The Pond would ever be discovered. To his mind, the perfect intelligence agency was a closed system, with all information flowing in and none out. He intended to seal all records that he kept, passing them down to whoever eventually replaced him, but never to allow the original documentation to be seen. It was pure luck that the cache found in Virginia was not destroyed when the agency was dissolved and absorbed into the CIA in the 1950s, even if they were not passed into the care of that agency as they were supposed to be.

Ultimately, it would be The Pond's policy of absolute secrecy that led to its demise. The majority of the crucial work that the organisation did during the war remained a secret long past the end of the war, and for this reason, when congressional oversight came along, they essentially had nothing to show for themselves. In fact, most people didn't even believe that The Pond existed until Grombach was forced to come out and make a public statement about its work and achievements. By then, their operational budget had been slashed, and much of the usual operations had to be halted as The Pond no longer had the money to invest in foreign businesses to use as de facto embassies in hostile states. The last few operations that they conducted were marred by allegations of insufficient evidence being presented, primarily because of Grombach's outright refusal to share any information about the work it was doing. Sources could not be checked or verified because The Pond would not disclose its sources.

Grombach himself was absorbed into the CIA as the ongoing leader of The Pond's operations and the sole beneficiary of so many spy networks worldwide that would not trust in a new liaison. However, he found himself surrounded by enemies on all sides. Some questioned his professionalism because of his refusal to share information. Others felt like he was a mad dog set loose in the agency as he scurried about trying to find evidence of spies among them. To make matters worse, a great many of the CIA agents were holdovers from the OSS – a much beloved institution that Grombach's Pond had effectively destroyed with its reports of communist spies within it.

By 1955, The Pond's final subsidiary form was also destroyed. All of the operations that Grombach disclosed to his new superiors had been taken over by the mainstream CIA, and Grombach himself had become so embittered by the destruction of his brainchild that he began using his position to spitefully report those same superiors and co-workers as Communist sympathisers, just because they had crossed him. His reputation was in tatters, leading to much questioning of just how much of his secretive work had merely been the result of guesswork and ego. The efforts of The Pond were more or less overlooked by history up until that point, so having it fade away in such a manner seemed almost appropriate. It was an ignominious end to an agency that had been integral to not only the war effort but a great deal of America's anti-communist activities abroad in the years following the war. Specifics of The Pond's operations are still secret, even now that disclosure of sealed documents from WW2 is underway, due to the way that it was operated. However, it has been possible to ascertain that, without The Pond, there would have been no Operation Paperclip, and the resultant space programme that grew out of the Nazi rocketry expertise. Likewise, the entire course of the war would likely have been changed if it had not come to America's attention that the Axis Powers were searching Scandinavia for the rare materials required for their nuclear weapons programme. Another operation that can have its success directly attributed to The Pond's counter-espionage efforts.

So the question then becomes, whose side was Marcel Petiot on?

Assuming that our prior assertions are correct, and that he was working with the Abwehr prior to WW2 in exchange for a pension from them, then it is safe to assume that his declarations of patriotism after WW1 were all patently false. Unless we follow the logic that the previously aggrieved Petiot put aside his grudge against the French government after his ill use on the front lines in WW1, or that his hatred of the Germans outweighed the money that he was receiving from them. A final alternative is, of course, that he was encouraged to reach out to his WW1 German contacts by his new employers at The Pond so that he might gain access to intelligence from them as a double agent.

The truth is most likely that Marcel Petiot held loyalty only to Marcel Petiot. That when the Germans were paying him, he worked for them, and when The Pond came along offering him even more money for doing essentially the same work in duplicate, he was happy to share what he knew with everyone who brought some cash to the table. It would be entirely in keeping with his other sociopathic tendencies for him to care nothing about the morality of his actions, or about his loyalties, when there was a possibility of profit on the line. It is equally possible that he, like most people at the time, had no idea which way the war was going to turn out, and he was doing his damnedest to make sure that he had a friend in every camp who would vouch for him when the dust settled. Between the destruction of the Gestapo and Abwehr records and the level of secrecy employed by The Pond, it is likely that we will never know the truth of his career as a spy. Only that he was one. And that his contributions to the war effort helped to bring about the 20th century as we know it.

Who Was Doctor Satan?

It is difficult to hold both ideas in our mind at the same time: That Marcel Petiot was a psychopathic murderer motivated exclusively by his greed and advancement, and that Marcel Petiot was an agent of an American spy network that may have saved the world from Fascist rule or nuclear annihilation. A boy who intently read every book that was put in front of him and had the kind of blazing intellect that let him study to be a practicing doctor in little more than a year. Conversely, a boy who tried to sexually assault and murder his classmates for his own amusement, who was flung from one special education facility to the next because nobody could tame him. A successful doctor, husband, and mayor, who also happened to be a depraved mass murderer who cut the fingers from corpses so that he could steal their wedding rings. Within Marcel, we find the ultimate dichotomy of man. The elevated angel of our better nature and the debased beast of our past.

The courtroom was the perfect place to see how Marcel operated, despite the whole world knowing about his crimes.

Despite the certainty of judges, jurors and the audience that he was guilty, by weaving lies and striking out with his charming yet incisive wit, Marcel Petiot won people over.

By now you have seen the litany of crimes that we are certain that he committed, and have heard the accusations of so many more that were never proven but seem almost invariably to have been his work. You have seen him lie, cheat, defraud, rob, poison and butcher the most vulnerable and desperate of people in the worst of all possible circumstances. Yet for all of that, there is no denying that he contributed to the world in positive ways too. Certainly, his pursuit of a career in medicine was not born out of a desire to help others, but there can be no denying that he performed his tasks ably and cured many of their ailments. Similarly, his career as a spy was almost certainly rooted in a desire for personal gain, but the net results of his actions contributed to the Allies winning World War 2 and mankind reaching the moon. Even though there is no denying that he was a fundamentally evil man, he still made a positive contribution to the world. It in no way balances the moral scales, of course, but it is still fascinating to see a real-life Ayn Rand hero functioning in much the way that she described in her pseudo-philosophical works. Being entirely self-serving, but somehow improving the world as a result.

If you look at Marcel Petiot from the perspective of his wife, then he was simply a busy man who worked all hours of the day to provide his family with a luxurious lifestyle, precisely the sort of man that any young woman with a desire for comfort might seek out.

If you look at him from the perspective of one of his patients, he was a brusque doctor much more interested in getting them in and out of the door as swiftly as possible than in making the polite small talk that they had come to expect.

Were you to consider him from the perspective of the criminals that he associated with, then you might see a genius of your art with the conviction and courage to perform more daring feats than anyone that you had ever encountered before. If you were a part of the Fly-Tox network, you might see a Resistance hero, or the man who had blackmailed you into taking on the dangerous task of spying upon the most feared branch of the Nazi state apparatus.

All in all, Marcel's carefully partitioned life leaves nobody with a full perspective of the whole man. The only one who probably ever fully understood both the mask and the creature beneath it was the mistress that he murdered back when he was still Mayor of Villeneuve-sur-Yonne. She saw him at his most suave and charismatic, in the bloom of his youth when he still had all the fire of the man who had brought the fight to the German lines alone. She saw him as a leader and a doctor and a genius. Then when the truth threatened to out, and he saw more advantage in a world without her in it, she saw his savagery, his willingness to do whatever was necessary to get his way, the cold, calculating lizard brain that decided who lived and who died depending upon how easy it would make his life. Of everyone, Henrietta Debauve was the only person to see it all. Yet even she could not have comprehended the full breadth of the creature that beat her to death, then set her alight. She had never seen him on the field of battle or sneaking around dark alleys in the dead of night, hunting down Gestapo patrols. She had not seen him send out spies to identify enemies of France, and then use their connections to the Gestapo to blackmail them. Within Marcel, there was an infinite capacity for greatness and evil, and he did his best every day to fulfil them both.

Was Marcel mentally ill? Almost certainly. His hoarding of wealth went beyond greed and into compulsion. He had little to no impulse control, and it was only his position in the upper echelons of society that allowed him to pass unseen through the world despite the chaos that followed in his footsteps.

Was Marcel so mentally ill that he cannot be considered culpable for his actions? In a modern court, an insanity defence for Marcel's murders would likely be attempted. With his history of mental illness and violent outbursts, there is a strong argument to be made that some of his actions could have been accounted for by his sickly mind. However, the scale of his operations in Paris, the volume of bodies being processed in the charnel house that he had set up exclusively for such a project, the network of confidantes and allies that he had amassed to make his wholesale slaughter of fleeing refugees possible, all of these things were carefully calculated and planned. He may have set off down the course of murder and robbery on an impulse, but he remained there because he judged it to be the most profitable path.

There are some people, particularly in more liberal circles, who no longer believe that the word evil is appropriate. They concede that people do bad things, but they ascribe reasons to those actions: past traumas or economic pressures that drive a person to commit actions beyond the scope of usual morality. Marcel Petiot was highly educated, wealthy and almost every moment in his life that he suffered was as a direct result of his actions. Every day, he woke up, and he chose violence. He could have lived out his life in comfort and luxury with what he made as a doctor, but it was not enough for him.

Nothing was ever enough for him. He had to have more than everyone else. More than his father. More than his brother. More than anyone that he met in the street. He had to be more than everyone else. A doctor who had studied in the finest institutions. A mayor so beloved that a whole council quit in protest of his investigation for corruption. A leader of the Resistance so devoted to the cause that he worked day and night against the Nazi regime. A spy, who worked all sides and shaped the 20th century into a future that nobody mired in the fog of war could ever have predicted. A genius, crafting secret weapons. An assassin, destroying the Reich in the dead of night. A saboteur, planting bombs and turning the tide of the war. The emperor of crime. The devil himself.

He was so intent upon his own aggrandisement that he had to craft a legend around himself so that even centuries into the future, people would still be speaking his name in hushed tones.

There can be no denying that he was successful in being remembered, if nothing else. How many of the true Resistance leaders in occupied France are still remembered today? How many of those brave patriots who did whatever they had to do to drive out the occupying Nazis can you name right now, other than Marcel Petiot, who evidence still cannot confirm as having any part in the Resistance whatsoever.

So yes, Marcel Petiot was a doctor and a killer and a soldier and a politician and a husband and a father and a fighter and a lover and a thief and a madman and a genius and a hero and a monster and a psychopath and everything else that a man could be, but there can be no denying that he earned his Nom de Guerre. For who else in all of human history could be called something like Doctor Satan without there being any sense of hyperbole whatsoever?

Only Marcel Petiot.

Want More?

Did you enjoy *Doctor Satan* and want some more True Crime?

YOUR FREE BOOK IS WAITING

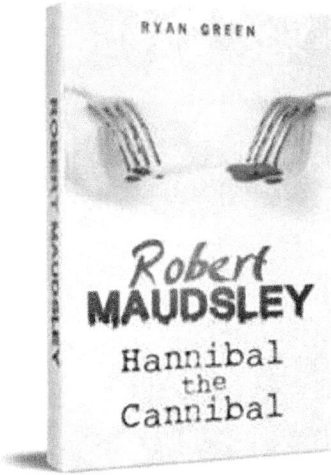

From bestselling author Ryan Green

There is a man who is officially classed as "**Britain's most dangerous prisoner**"

The man's name is Robert Maudsley, and his crimes earned him the nickname "**Hannibal the Cannibal**"

This free book is an exploration of his story...

amazonkindle nook kobo iBooks

★ ★ ★ ★ ★ *"Ryan brings the horrifying details to life. I can't wait to read more by this author!"*

Get a free copy of ***Robert Maudsley: Hannibal the Cannibal*** when you sign up to join my Reader's Group.

www.ryangreenbooks.com/free-book

Every Review Helps

If you enjoyed the book and have a moment to spare, I would really appreciate a short review on Amazon. Your help in spreading the word is gratefully received and reviews make a huge difference to helping new readers find me. Without reviewers, us self-published authors would have a hard time!

Type in your link below to be taken straight to my book review page.

US	geni.us/dsUS
UK	geni.us/dsUK
Australia	geni.us/dsAUS
Canada	geni.us/dsCAN

Thank you! I can't wait to read your thoughts.

About the Author

Ryan Green is a true crime author who lives in Herefordshire, England with his wife, three children, and two dogs. Outside of writing and spending time with his family, Ryan enjoys walking, reading and windsurfing.

Ryan is fascinated with History, Psychology and True Crime. In 2015, he finally started researching and writing his own work and at the end of the year, he released his first book on Britain's most notorious serial killer, Harold Shipman.

He has since written several books on lesser-known subjects, and taken the unique approach of writing from the killer's perspective. He narrates some of the most chilling scenes you'll encounter in the True Crime genre.

You can sign up to Ryan's newsletter to receive a free book, updates, and the latest releases at:

WWW.RYANGREENBOOKS.COM

More Books by Ryan Green

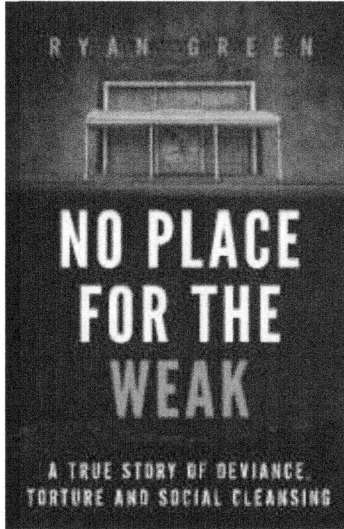

On 20 May 1999, the South Australian Police were called to investigate a disused bank in the unassuming town of Snowtown, in connection to the disappearance of multiple missing people. The Police were not prepared for the chilling scene that awaited them.

The officers found six barrels within the abandoned bank vault, each filled with acid and the remains of eight individuals. Accompanying the bodies were numerous everyday tools that pathologists would later confirm were used for prolonged torture, murder and cannibalism.

The findings shocked Australia to its core, which deepened still when it was revealed that the torture and murders were committed by not one, but a group of killers. The four men, led by John Bunting, targeted paedophiles, homosexuals, addicts or the 'weak' in an attempt to cleanse society.

More Books by Ryan Green

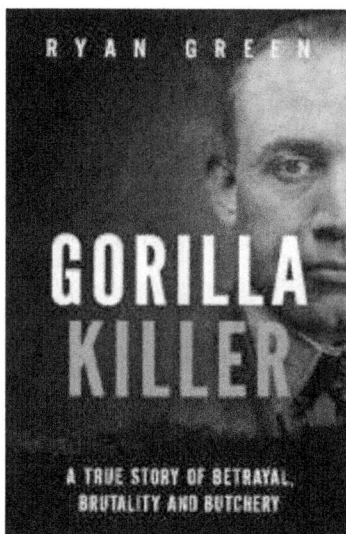

On 20th February 1926, landlady Clara Newman (60) opened her door to a potential tenant who enquired into the availability of one of her rooms. Despite his grim and bulky appearance, he introduced himself politely, in a soft-spoken voice whilst clutching a Bible in one of his large hands. She invited him in. The moment he stepped into her home, he lunged forwards, wrapping his over-sized fingers around her throat and forced her to the ground. She couldn't scream. He had learned the dangers of a scream. She slowly slipped into darkness. Given what would follow, it was probably a kindness.

The 'Gorilla Killer', Earle Nelson, roamed over 7,000 miles of North America undetected, whilst satisfying his deranged desires. During a span of almost two years, he choked the life out of more than twenty unsuspecting women, subjected their bodies to the most unspeakable acts, and seemingly enjoyed the process.

More Books by Ryan Green

On 23 January 1978, David Wallin returned to an unlit home. His pregnant wife, Teresa (22), was nowhere to be seen. The radio was still playing and there were some peculiar stains on the carpet. Wallin nervously followed the stains to his bedroom and encountered a scene so chilling that it would haunt him for the rest of his life. Teresa had been sexually assaulted and mutilated. She was also missing body parts and large volumes of blood.

Four days later, the Sacramento Police Department were called to a home approximately a mile away from the Wallin residence. They were not prepared for the horror that awaited them. Daniel Meredith (56) and Jason Miroth (6) were shot multiple times. Evelyn Miroth (38) was disfigured, disembowelled and abused like Teresa. She was also missing body parts and large quantities of blood. David Ferreira (2), who Evelyn was babysitting, was nowhere to be seen and likely in the hands of the deranged mass murderer.

More Books by Ryan Green

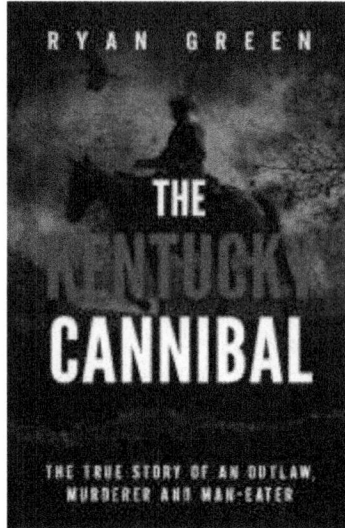

In 1850, following a divorce and a number of encounters with the law, Boone Helm headed 'Out West' to chase the Californian Gold Rush with his cousin. When his cousin pulled out at the last minute, Helm was incensed, and brutally stabbed him to death. Helm was detained in an asylum for the mentally disturbed but managed to escape.

Helm continued his journey west with renewed vigour, where he opportunistically killed and consumed the flesh of adversaries and travelling companions, earning him the nickname 'The Kentucky Cannibal'. After several brutal months in the wilderness, he finally made it California. At a time where violence was the law of the land, Helm's savage set of skills could finally be recognised and rewarded.

Free True Crime Audiobook

Listen to four chilling True Crime stories in one collection. Follow the link below to download a FREE copy of *The Ryan Green True Crime Collection: Vol. 3.*

WWW.RYANGREENBOOKS.COM/FREE-AUDIOBOOK

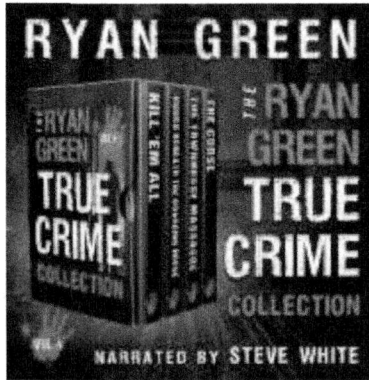

"Ryan Green has produced another excellent book and belongs at the top with true crime writers such as M. William Phelps, Gregg Olsen and Ann Rule" –**B.S. Reid**

"Wow! Chilling, shocking and totally riveting! I'm not going to sleep well after listening to this but the narration was fantastic. Crazy story but highly recommend for any true crime lover!" –**Mandy**

"Torture Mom by Ryan Green left me pretty speechless. The fact that it's a true story is just...wow" –**JStep**

"Graphic, upsetting, but superbly read and written" –**Ray C**

WWW.RYANGREENBOOKS.COM/FREE-AUDIOBOOK

Printed in Great Britain
by Amazon

25626660R00088